EUROPEAN FARM COMMUNITIES FOR AUTISM

by

JANE J. GIDDAN, M.A.

ASSOCIATE PROFESSOR
OF CLINICAL PSYCHIATRY
MEDICAL COLLEGE OF OHIO

and

NORMAN S. GIDDAN, Ph.D.

CLINICAL PROFESSOR
OF PSYCHIATRY
MEDICAL COLLEGE OF OHIO

MEDICAL COLLEGE OF OHIO PRESS
TOLEDO, OHIO

Printed in the United States of America.

Medical College of Ohio Press, Box 10008, Toledo, OH 43699-0001.

Cover design by Marshall Andrews.
Cover illustration by Bronwen Shea.
Printed by BookMasters, Inc.

Library of Congress Cataloging-in-Publication Data

Giddan, Jane J.
    European farm communitites for autism / by Jane J. Giddan and
    Norman S. Giddan.
        p. cm.
    Includes bibliographical references (p.) and index.
    ISBN 0-944742-04-1
    1. Autism—Patients—Rehabilitation—Europe.   2. Therapeutic
communities—Europe.   3. Agriculture—Europe—Therapeutic use.
I. Giddan, Norman S.   II. Title.
RC553.A88G53   1993
616.89'8203'094—dc20   93-31248
                                                                CIP

EUROPEAN
FARM COMMUNITIES
FOR AUTISM

Contents

Preface

For a variety of reasons, an increasing worldwide population of adults with autism is being identified. The disorder is being diagnosed earlier as awareness of its characteristics spreads; with better care individuals with autism are living into adulthood; and many institutions in developed nations that once warehoused people with developmental disabilities have now emptied their wards and released these people to the care of their communities (see Dawson, 1989; Gillberg, 1989). As a result, there is increasing involvement of family and parent associations. The new situation raises critical questions: How and where should adolescents and adults with autism live and work? What models are effective? Which arrangements have not yet been tried?

Several models have been created in the United States within the last few years, but Western Europeans have a wider range of programs in operation. The purpose of our study was to visit and survey a variety of model programs throughout Europe, to compare and contrast them, then to disseminate information about these programs and thereby increase the pool of service options in the United States, Europe, and elsewhere. The programs surveyed were nominated by parent associations, Autism-Europe, and professionals serving clientele with autism.

Since the Europeans have put their efforts into planning and development of programs and published little detailed information about them, we hope our visits to their non-urban communities for adults with autism, networking between those centers, and this monograph itself will be of value to them, too. Our goal is to increase the variety and improve the effectiveness of services for adolescents and adults with autism and their families—the consumers.

In the U.S.A. large state institutions for those with mental retardation historically have been the dumping grounds for individuals with autism who could no longer be cared for at home by their families. With little individual assistance in large institutions, the behaviors of those with autistic disorders deteriorated, with self-stimulating or ritualistic activities increasing to the point that these adults became minimally functional and totally dependent on caretakers. It should be emphasized, too, that this was not the fate of adults at all institutions.

The large-scale de-institutionalization of the last fifteen years in the U.S.A. has brought the return of many individuals with serious disabilities to the community. Programs have been created in urban environments incorporating group homes, supervised apartments, and job coaches in work settings. In more rural areas, the farmstead model has been pioneered, offering both residential and vocational opportunities. The non-urban farmstead, Bittersweet Farms, has been successfully established and is serving as a model for efforts in many other states. It was inspired by the program at Somerset Court in England more than fifteen years ago. Adaptations of this model in various American states such as North Carolina and Ohio assimilate the interests and abilities of residents with autism as well as the talents of staff, not to mention the increasing interest in the farmstead philosophy. Within both urban and non-urban models an important emphasis is on integrating adults with autism into the larger community. Schopler and Hennike (1990) have also reminded us that the notion of community services is no automatic panacea:

> . . . dumping handicapped people into the community under the deinstitutionalization banner, armed only with a paper bag filled with miscellaneous belongings, can easily seal a fate worse than institutional life. In parallel we have learned from some small, community-based group homes located in a hostile neighborhood, staffed by underqualified personnel, that they have the same potential for sterility, isolation, and neglect found in the largest custodial institutions. (p. 296)

Several models are now in place in America, but experimental programs abroad are apparently breaking new ground. A variety of centers for adults with autism are now in place throughout Europe, and efforts are being made by the International Association of Autism Europe to create a viable network among them.

From correspondence (see Appendix B) with leaders of autism societies, program directors, and other professionals in Western Europe, Britain, Ireland, and Israel, we have learned that the range, quality, and innovativeness of European settings exceed that which we have here. England seems to have the broadest and most creative spectrum of living and working arrangements including rural farmstead programs, small homes, and entire villages which serve individuals with many kinds of handicapping conditions. Professionals and parents in Ireland, Britain, Denmark, Germany, Italy, Spain, Holland, France and Belgium point to one or two successful non-urban centers and hope to build more. Other countries, such as those in Eastern Europe, are just beginning to recognize autistic disorders in young children and are beginning to understand that teaching and training options are available.

The senior author visited two non-urban communities in Denmark and Holland and was able to develop detailed information about them, and to compare them to each other and to the farmstead model here in the States. The other farmsteads presented here were studied through interviews, surveys, letters, and phone calls. As far as possible, we wanted them to tell their own stories (see Patton & Westby, 1992). Our goal was to have at least qualitative data on the processes, staff, and perceived effectiveness of some of the major programs in the British Isles and Western Europe. The fundamental objectives, therefore, were to identify, study, and describe outstanding models of non-urban living and working communities for adults with autism in those countries.

This participatory action research method (Chesler, 1991) documented the visits to two settings with audio tape recordings of interviews with staff members, family representatives, and some residents. Visits were to Ny Allerødgård in Denmark and Wolfheze of the Dr. Leo Kannerhuis program in Holland. The material gathered from this first-hand experience greatly exceeded that which could be collected through the surveys alone. A large portion of the material gathered on Le Pradelle in France was obtained through several hours of personal interviews with Mme. Françoise Grémy during the Autism-Europe 4th Congress at The Hague. Our work reflects these inequities and in no way suggests any qualitative or evaluative distinction among the settings.

Pre-visit preparations included:

a) Correspondence with individuals (professionals, administrators, parents) active in the field of autism in the United States and Europe, as well as communication with autism societies in various European countries in order to identify appropriate sites.
b) Letters and telephone calls to identify several sites to establish a schedule for visitations.
c) A "protocol" agreeable to each site and the participation and cooperation of Center directors, staff, parents, families, and residents with regard to completing the protocol.

Programs and policies to be evaluated and studied included:

a) Programs and treatment philosophy, goals, and effectiveness.
b) Staff selection and training.
c) Views, involvement and participation of parents, family members, and friends.
d) Relationships of residents to community life.
e) Role of self-help and social support processes vis-à-vis centers, families and residents.

We hope that state and federal government departments which continue to mandate least restrictive educational opportunities for all individuals with disabilities will clearly benefit, too, from this new source of program models. Those taking responsibility for the continuing care and teaching of adults with autism need behavioral research and program evaluation to help provide a larger and more effective range of program formats than now exist in the U.S.—including urban group homes, various-sized institutions, ranches, and non-urban farmsteads. Additional groups seeking such information include active family organizations, regional and state societies, and national groups concerned about autism. There is interest as well in other forums whose concerns are for individuals with related or similar severely disabling conditions.

To identify and locate the settings we visited and studied, we were provided with information from many organizations. Our thanks go to the World Health Organization, the World Federation for Mental Health, and the International Association Autism Europe. They directed us to the national autism societies and key individuals in each of the European countries.

We are grateful to American and international colleagues and pen-pals, who provided such useful and timely correspondence: Mrs. Chanita Rodney of ENOSH, the Israel Mental Health Association; Mrs. Leah Rabin of the Israeli Society for Autistic Children; Dr. Anna Balász of Hungary; Ms. Sybil Elgar and Mrs. Edith Morgan of Britain; Christiane Baltaxe, Ph.D., of the U.C.L.A. Neuropsychiatric Institute; and Jaak Panksepp, Ph.D., of Bowling Green State University.

Our special appreciation goes to so many who gave generously of their time, who provided personal attention, and whose thoughtful contributions to this project helped transform our dreams into reality: From Britain we thank Paul Shattock of the Autism Research Unit, University of Sunderland; from Brussels, Mrs. Maria Hoffman, Secretary General of the International Association Autism Europe; and from the U.S., Bernard Rimland, Ph.D., founder of the Autism Research Institute in San Diego. Dr. Rimland gave us permission to reprint two editorials on residential alternatives from the *Autism Research Review International* as the basis of his prologue.

The personal contacts we made brought to life the history and evolution of each farmstead center. For their unmatched hospitality and warm generosity we thank our colleagues in Denmark—Mogens Andersen, Berit Skovmand, Martin Harris, Gugu and Ernst Kristoffersen, Demetrious Haracopos and the staff and residents at Ny Allerødgård.

We say a similar thank-you with unlimited gratitude to Anneke van Belle-Bakker, Egbert Reÿnen, Wim Kemperman, Kees Otten, Anita Verstraten, Charles Laumen, Irene v.d. Pol, Hank and Magrite Dokter and the staff and residents at Dr. Leo Kannerhuis and Wolfheze in the Netherlands.

Madame François Grémy of France was most forthcoming and generous with her intelligence and energy, and provided information along with Monsieur Lionel Bourdely and Dr. Pierre Borrelly.

We appreciate the contribution of Pat and Nuala Matthews of the Irish Society for Autism and Pat Shannon, manager of the Dunfirth Community.

From Spain we thank Juan Roca i Miralles, Jordi Oliver i Ros, and their families, as well as Francesc Cuxart i Fina.

We acknowledge our appreciation for the substantial contributions of Christopher Atkins of Britain, Hermann Cordes of Germany and Raphael Ferri, M.D., of OASI in Italy.

Information was provided from each of the participating European centers through surveys (sample in Appendix C), written correspondence, and personal interviews. We were deeply moved by the dedication, courage, honesty, and thoroughness mirrored by the materials shared with us and have tried to present them as accurately as possible in this text.

It was gratifying for the senior author to be part of the first gathering of leaders of these farm communities May 7, 1992, at the 4th Congress Autism-Europe in the Hague. It was there that the idea of an International Network was born.

For their conscientious assistance in translation of documents from French, German, Danish, Dutch, and Spanish into English, we are grateful to Gabrielle Giddan, Caroline Balcon, Sarah Wenzinger, Ingeborg Karolak, Carin Allen, Mies Reyerse, Martha Delgado, and Lourdes Santiago.

For word processing assistance in correspondence and for patient work on this manuscript, our gratitude goes to

Laura Pietras, Karen Nino, Amy Bettinger, and Teresa Shiffert. We also greatly appreciate the editing skills of Linda Smith, Ph.D.

The Department of Psychiatry at the Medical College of Ohio generously provided funding for this research project, the surveys, and associated travel. We are deeply appreciative of the nurture and support of Joel P. Zrull, M.D., Chairman, without whose encouragement this project could not have been initiated or completed.

Finally, we want to recognize the genuine goodwill of Mr. Lawrence J. Burns, Mr. Ashel G. Bryan and William E. McMillen, Ph.D.

JJG and NSG
Toledo, Ohio
U.S.A.
June, 1993

Prologue

Bernard Rimland, Ph.D.[1]

I am pleased to be invited to contribute to this volume on European farm communities for autistic adults. As the parent of a now-36 year old autistic son, I have been involved in the world of autism, in many ways, for many years. Until recently, however, I have not been involved except very superficially, in any aspect of residential living for autistic persons. However, here in the U.S., and I imagine it is also true to some extent in Europe as well, there has arisen a dangerous, militant movement of ideologically-motivated, self-appointed "advocates" who are convinced that they, and only they, know what is right for handicapped people, and who believe that their views must prevail for **all** of the handicapped. They are so committed to their ideological beliefs that they have no concern that their beliefs often run counter to scientific evidence. "Evidence and reason be damned" seems to be their motto. They will use any means, fair or foul, to prevail over those who might disagree with them. They are very much like other political extremists, not only in their single-minded dedication to promoting their ideology, but because they attempt to control other people's thinking by insisting that everyone use "politically correct" language. I refer to these people as "advozealots"—zealots who pose as advocates.

These advozealots, who really are advocates for their ideology and not for the handicapped, base their demands on what they hold to be the civil rights of the handicapped, as though those of us who disagree with them, who are often

[1]Dr. Rimland is Director of the Autism Research Institute, San Diego, California, U.S.A.

the parents of handicapped persons, have no concern for the civil rights of our children.

Every person is a unique individual, differing in many important ways from everyone else. What is good and appropriate for one person—autistic or not—may be wrong for another. These details are of no concern to the advozealots.

There are a number of issues on which I and many other informed and concerned people differ with the advozealots, but the issue that concerns us here is residential living. The advozealots insist that the handicapped must live in small urban apartments or group homes. Period.

Be on guard to protect your loved ones from the destructive intentions of those who pose as friends, protectors and "advocates."

Community, My Foot!

Many months have passed since the vicious, unprovoked beating of motorist Rodney King by members of the L.A. Police Department first appeared on our TV screens. Most of us have seen the replays so often that we can summon them to our mind's eye without the benefit of electronic equipment.

The Rodney King affair unleashed a storm of public outrage and protest. Cries for reform were widely heard and many suggestions for improving police accountability, in Los Angeles and elsewhere, were made. Some reforms have been adopted. Despite the highly emotionally charged situation, there were, so far as I know, no calls for the total abolition of the Los Angeles Police Department, nor the abolition of other police departments elsewhere, where similar incidents have since surfaced. It is widely understood and accepted that even though there are instances of abuse, police departments perform an important and necessary social function, and the good they do far outweighs the bad.

Contrast the above situation with what has occurred during the past several decades with regard to "mental" institutions. Historically, people with serious mental incapacities such as schizophrenia, severe retardation, or autism were left to wander the streets of cities and towns, defending themselves as best they could from attack by others, scrounging food from wherever they could find it, including the gutter, trying to find shelter from cold and snow. To create a safe and humane environment for these unfortunate individuals, society created asylums—places of safety and refuge—far better than living the life of homeless and despised vagrants on the streets. Many of these institutional asylums did a wonderful job. Others did a very poor job, and permitted terrible abuse and neglect of the residents to occur.

Along came television. Guess what? The public was not treated to the spectacle of clean, well fed and well treated mental patients basking in the sun or participating in exercise classes in well equipped gyms. Instead the public was shown the worst of the "snake pits." *Christmas in Purgatory,* and the horrible revelations about patients' lives at Willowbrook, were presented to national audiences. This of course is to be expected, and is in fact a good thing, because it exposed problems that require reforms and led to the establishment of state and federal guidelines. But it gave a very distorted picture of the true situation. How much national media coverage would have been given to secretly videotaped images of LAPD officers helping little old ladies across the street?

The exposés of neglect and abuse at some institutions led to an indiscriminate smearing of the reputations of all institutions everywhere, and a concerted effort to get patients out of institutions into what is euphemistically called "the community."

The deinstitutionalization movement took hold with a vengeance. Countless thousands of people who are unable to cope with the problems of survival in a harsh and uncaring society were dumped into the streets, or into small, privately run facilities, under the supposed protection and care of a large number of expensive, but inadequate and ineffective, "*community* mental health centers."

Deinstitutionalization proved to be a cure worse than the disease. At least five books have been published in the past three years detailing its tragic consequences. Seymour Sarason of Yale University, one of the leaders of the deinstitutionalization movement in the U.S., describes these efforts in his recent autobiography, *The Making of an American Psychologist*. He concludes that the most serious professional mistake of his life was his advocacy of deinstitutionalization. (I tip my hat to you, Dr. Sarason. Few of us have the courage and integrity to own up to our mistakes.)

As the legions of poorly fed, physically and mentally ill homeless persons on our streets attest, moving people out into that wonderfully warm and nurturing "community" wasn't necessarily a bright idea. Some of the institutions they left were excellent places; others were terrible. Some of the community places they were moved to were excellent; others were terrible.

If abuse and neglect are going to occur, they can occur far more easily and more secretly in small group homes in the community than they can in a major institution with many other people present. Group homes can come and go very rapidly. Some last many years; others last only months. It is not unknown for the residents of such homes to be left on the street when the owner of the facility decides that he or she can no longer tolerate the stress of trying to find enough semi-qualified, minimum-pay, high-turnover workers to care for the residents.

The word "community" needs careful examination. It derives from "common," and implies a degree of coherence, shared interests and concerns that are today rarely found in urban environments. The word "community" conjures an image of a white-haired grandmotherly lady at one's door, asking, "Can you use this freshly baked apple pie? We just have too many apples this year." When was the last time this happened in your neighborhood? Many group homes in the U.S. are located in places that would be better described as urban jungles than communities. I am aware of group homes in areas that are so dangerous that the social workers will visit them only in pairs—on those rare occasions when there is any supervision at all. I am aware of institutions where real community, caring people, long-term relationships, exist in abundance.

Community once implied human relatedness. Now it refers merely to an urban area. Community living—with no other options—is an ideology pushed with religious fervor by the sanctimonious but misguided Association for Persons with Severe Handicaps (TASH). I read with grim amusement the complaint in their most recent newsletter: "Although persons with severe disabilities have been living in the community physically for some time, they have not generally been participating in the shared life of those communities." What shared life? Community, my foot!

Let us not be misled by the warm fuzzy feeling that the word "community" is intended to instill. Let us not be misled into the feeling of abandonment and neglect that the word "institution" has come to connote. I am in touch with literally thousands of parents of autistic children and adults throughout the world. Many of these children are maintained in healthy, happy and to them and their parents, satisfying environments on farms and ranches and in institutions, public and private, that parents do not want to see closed or abandoned.

While many, perhaps most, urban group homes are excellent, I disagree strongly with those who insist that urban group homes must be the *only* residential option. I favor the existence of a variety of options to fit different family and individual needs and preferences. We need not only urban group homes but rural residences, such as farms and ranches. And we need institutions—good, well-run institutions—for some of our sons and daughters.

I believe with the proper technology all kinds of residential facilities can be run in safe and responsible ways. Both small group homes and large institutions could be monitored frequently by randomly scheduled surprise drop-in visits from inspectors employed by advocacy groups, rather than by the organization running the group home or institution. Monitoring by electronic surveillance provides another means of protection.

I recently advocated the availability of farm and ranch residences for autistic individuals, non-urban alternatives such as Bittersweet Farms or Rusty's Morningstar Ranch (and I shall do it again, here). For many months afterward, and even to this day, I receive enthusiastic letters from parents who want that option available for their children when they are no longer here to care for them. That rural option, the urban group home option, and the state institutional option should all be available so families can exercise freedom of choice.

The Non-Urban Alternative

Like most parents of autistic adults, my wife and I are often asked what long-term plans we have for Mark, our autistic son. Mark has always lived with us, in our home. Like most parents of autistic adults, we have given Mark's future long and careful consideration. Unlike most parents of autistic adults, I have had the opportunity to visit a vast number of facilities for autistic people, have talked and corresponded with many thousands of parents and professionals, and have read much of what has been written about autism for over thirty years.

Before sharing my thoughts with you, let me emphasize something we all know, but nevertheless often overlook: not only are you and I very different; our children differ markedly from each other as well.

Given our "druthers," my wife and I feel that Mark's future would be happiest, most meaningful and productive, on a farm or ranch with similarly handicapped peers and companions.

A dozen years ago Mark, then twenty-two, spent part of the summer at the farm operated by Benhaven in Connecticut. He loved it, and talks about it to this day. Feeding the chickens, collecting the eggs, planting, watering, gathering vegetables for sale and for the table was meaningful, productive work to Mark. Farming has been meaningful and productive work for the vast majority of mankind for hundreds of generations, since farming was invented some sixty centuries ago. Mark returned home fit, tan, and healthy. He takes pride today in reporting the growth and ripening of the tomatoes, cucumbers, lettuce, and squash he tends carefully in our backyard garden.

There are a number of farms and ranches for autistic adults and teenagers in various places in the U.S. as, of course, in other countries. Perhaps the best known is Bittersweet Farms in Ohio. The recently published book,

Autistic Adults at Bittersweet Farms, provides a great deal of invaluable why, what, and how information about Bittersweet Farms and related settings.

Similar communities are being developed in North Carolina, California, and elsewhere. In the Netherlands, the Dr. Leo Kannerhuis houses twenty adolescents with autism. Four houses, each accommodating between four and six residents, are located near a workshop and a farmyard on the grounds of a hospital. Residents work a five-hour day at greenhouse and farming chores, housework, poultry raising, gardening, caring for livestock, and keeping up the buildings.

Rusty's Morningstar Ranch in Arizona is a smaller, non-urban residential center for autistic young men, who learn and practice the art of ranching from experienced ranch hands. Jack and Carlene Armstrong established Rusty's Morningstar Ranch several years ago, when they concluded that the high stress of the rapidly growing city of Phoenix was much more than they could expect their autistic son, Rusty, to cope with.

There are five Camphill villages and schools in the U.S., and over fifty in Europe and Africa, dedicated to providing rural living and learning opportunities to the mentally handicapped. I am not personally aware of autistic residents of Camphill.

Appealing as they are to some, including our family, non-urban farm and ranch settings such as Bittersweet Farms and Rusty's Morningstar Ranch are met with disdain and strenuous objections from a small but vocal segment of parents and professionals. Their complaints, as I understand them, seem to be largely ideological in nature. They seem to feel that farm life somehow violates two catchwords currently in favor: "community" and "integration." Since farm and ranch communities have existed for centuries, I do not understand why this new concept of communities recognizes only those in urban settings, such as urban group homes— small urban group homes—as acceptable residences for adults handicapped by autism, retardation, and similar disabilities.

One nationally recognized educator refers to non-urban residences disparagingly as "funny farms," calling attention to the old (and intelligent, in my opinion) practice of placing handicapped persons out of harm's way, in low-stress rural settings, in what is usually a kinder, gentler environment.

Why a Farm?

I know many parents who are pleased with their adult son's or daughter's placement in a rural setting, just as I know many who are pleased with a placement in an urban group home. Why do my wife and I prefer a rural setting for our son? Here are some of our reasons:

1. Long-term security. Economic downturns and political budget-slashing are serious threats which rural residences seem intrinsically better able to survive. Here in California group homes (there are about 3,000!) open slowly, and often close quickly, sometimes without much warning. There have been cases in which group homes closed with no warning. A major concern to my wife and me is to protect our son from ever becoming one of the homeless street persons. A farm or ranch setting does not guarantee against such catastrophes, but to us does seem to offer significantly greater stability.

2. Safety/Stress. The increasingly stressful conditions of urban life, especially the high rate of violent crime, take their toll daily on even those of us considered normal. Being robbed, assaulted, lost, or even losing keys or missing a bus can be an immensely more traumatic event for the autistic person than for the rest of us. More than once Mark has returned home after a ride on the city bus, badly shaken by an encounter with an overzealous religionist, whose talk of sins and proffering of tracts were beyond Mark's comprehension. A non-urban environment seems to us to be much less dangerous, less stressful, and more forgiving.

3. Meaningful work. People's tastes and preferences vary enormously, but it seems to me that taking care of farm animals and growing vegetables are much more likely to be intrinsically understandable and rewarding than most of the kinds of jobs that are available in an urban setting. This is certainly so in Mark's case. Mark has compiled and stapled innumerable papers, stuffed innumerable envelopes,

licked and affixed countless stamps, and performed a great deal of other kinds of repetitive office work. He does it willingly, but he doesn't really like it, and considers it boring. Most of the jobs I'm aware of in sheltered workshops or in supported employment seem to us to be of similar sorts. We want Mark's life and work to be as rewarding as possible.

4. Congenial associates. Despite the great (inordinate?) popularity of the idea of integration, it is obvious to us that Mark, and many other handicapped people, are happiest, and feel most at home, among similarly handicapped people.

I am all too well aware of once happy handicapped individuals whose lives have been made miserable by their being "integrated" into a work situation, usually in a supported employment setting, where they feel isolated and excluded from the conversations and social activities of their non-handicapped co-workers. Imagine being dropped into a setting where people functioned at an intellectual level perhaps fifty or more IQ points above yours, where their comments, jokes, and conversations occurred on a level far above your capacity to comprehend, and where your infrequent inclusion into their activities and conversations was largely a function of their kindness and patience. Not very satisfactory—at least from our family's point of view.

The Need for Options

There are clearly pluses and minuses for each of the available options. The important point is that an increasing number of options are becoming available, so that concerned parents and guardians can begin to select the residential setting most appropriate to the autistic persons in their care. A dark cloud on the horizon concerns me, however. Those ideologically committed to the small urban group home exclusively may yet succeed in achieving their goal of outlawing, in one way or another, the options some families prefer. The Chaffee bill would have prevented federal funds from reaching residences, such as Bittersweet Farms, for fifteen or more handicapped persons. Not every residence with over fifteen beds is a Willowbrook; not every group home is a utopia. We must be wary of advocates who strive to close off options which are not to their personal liking.

La Pradelle
Saumane, France

The story of La Pradelle must begin with a brief consideration of France's autism societies and the psychoanalytic viewpoint. The French organization named La Fédération Sésame-Autism began in 1963 and by 1990 had evolved to include a national network of twenty-four affiliated regional associations, reaching 1200 families. Its goals are to unify families and address their needs, to advocate for the creation of specialized living establishments, to inform the public and political entities about autism, and to stimulate research and disseminate its results. Its publication, *Sésame,* appears four times a year reaching both parents and professionals.

The essential view of Sésame-Autism supports a multi-disciplinary approach (no approach is excluded) for the education, socialization, and care of those of all ages with autism, as long as their human rights are respected. It advocates for small centers, free-standing and unconnected to large institutions, based on one significant vocational focus that gives meaning to all individual and collective activities. In these centers, so-called "adapted work projects" (C.A.T.) are created which allow for production that will have significance and be of interest to each worker with autism.

Sésame-Autism has appropriately placed thirty individuals with autism each year and has contributed to reforming regulations in medical and educational centers for children with autism. It has also contributed to the report written by the Minister for the Handicapped on how to look after those with autism (Autism Europe Association, 1992). Medical and pedagogical research and the training of health and education professionals have been important goals as well.

In its efforts to expand services, Sésame-Autism has created twenty-one centers. "These include six day centers, and three special classes for children, nine residential centers, two centers where help is provided through work and two services to help adults" (Autism Europe Association, 1992, p. 20). There are future plans to open residential centers, one C.A.T., and one protected workshop. The largest regional associations within the Federation are Rhône-Alpes, Nord-Pas de Calais, Midi-Pyrénées, Paris, and Languedoc-Roussillon.

Among the other associations in France is Autism-Ile de France, set up in 1982 to group together families with autistic children, teenagers, or adults in the Paris region. It began with 224 members, most of them parents, and now has extended its membership throughout France. A non-profit organization, it is made up of an Administrative Council and an Executive Office, both composed mostly of parents.

The association's main objectives are to help families understand and bear the handicap of autism, and to inform political leaders and the public about autism. To foster dialogue between parents and professionals, it has helped set up the ARAPI association, a group which promotes research on autism and attempts to put parents and researchers in touch with each other.

The association publishes a quarterly newsletter for members, parents, and friends. It also organizes a large informational meeting on themes related to autism, which is open to the public. In the context of confused attitudes in France with regard to autism, it tries to develop all possible contacts with other associations and advocates for joint action on behalf of those with autism.

Sésame-Autism Languedoc-Roussillon is one of the three associations in southern France affiliated with the French Federation, Sésame-Autism. It has led a new movement which creates imaginative living and working environments for adults with autism, with a view toward continued growth in the future.

This new movement in France is emerging against the backdrop of a long history of psychoanalytic treatment for autism. Under the leadership of the Federation Sésame-

Autism, twelve communities have been created since 1987, serving a total of 200 residents. Françoise Grémy is now president of Sésame Autism Languedoc-Rousillon. When she began the association there in 1984, she was determined to remain open to all views of treatment, to create innovative new settings with a broad base of input. Consequently, the Board of Directors of Sésame-Autism Languedoc-Roussillon, includes parents, doctors, social workers, and educators. According to Mme. Grémy, their philosophy in creating the new communities has been "to offer persons suffering from autism and childhood psychosis, when they become adults, an interesting life, as similar as possible to everybody's life. This implies they are considered more as persons with possibilities than as people with various mental deficiencies."

The philosophy of La Pradelle is that life in a community and team work can break the isolation of their residents. Through work and leisure activities, communication can be reinforced both inside and beyond the centers. Access to language, spoken and written, is provided and concepts of time are emphasized in all settings.

Through the structure of real and meaningful work and a real salary, the creators of La Pradelle feel their workers gain a sense of security. Structure in the group homes is designed to extend that feeling. Efforts are made to avoid as much as possible all repetitive tasks which might generate or reinforce stereotyped behaviors of those with autism. Mme. Grémy explains:

> This is the main reason for the choice of a farm, with various activities, offering an understandable meaning; and for the choice of preparing food.

Mme. Grémy reflects on the historical psychoanalytic influences on the treatment of autism in France as well as on the current possibilities. About twenty-five years ago, children with autism were either kept at home or placed in psychiatric hospitals, but this is no longer true. Since about 1975 they can be enrolled in two kinds of institutions: Day Care Centers which are supported by the national health budget and Medical Social Institutions which are funded by the budget of social affairs. The latter has two levels, Medical Educational Institutions for the young children with autism and Medical Professional Institutions for those over age fourteen who are ready for some preparation for work.

Although some psychiatrists may still offer psychoanalytic-style verbal therapy, these children's institutions have added play activities and school programs provided by educators. Even psychiatric hospitals for adults in France have begun to evolve differently in recent years. They now have some flats in the community with therapeutic support, although these are rather scarce.

At the same time, Sésame-Autism has created alternative institutions for its specific population, diverging from the psychiatric hospital models and from the format of the C.A.T. institutions for those with mental retardation. Sheltered workshop-type activities like repetitive packaging of materials did not seem appropriate for their residents, so the founders of La Pradelle sought more imaginative projects. They have moved gradually from their psychoanalytic roots into the realm of behavioral treatment, but do not want to break the ties completely. In light of that Mme. Grémy observes:

> Even if my son has been taken into a psychoanalytic institution and he has improved, I don't say it is because it was psychoanalytic. Some people may say that it is in spite of it. I don't know, but there it is.

They continue to remain open to all treatment and educational approaches available—a kind of multi-theoretical viewpoint which also employs community and social support, like families and parents, to initiate, diversify, and stengthen the living and working environments for adolescents and adults with autism in France.

La Pradelle

La Pradelle began in 1987, at a time when settings for adults with autism were very rare. It includes three compo-

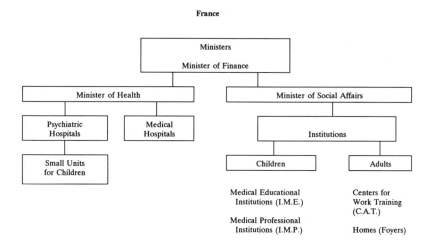

France

Ministers

Minister of Finance

Minister of Health

Minister of Social Affairs

Psychiatric Hospitals

Medical Hospitals

Institutions

Small Units for Children

Children

Adults

Medical Educational Institutions (I.M.E.)

Medical Professional Institutions (I.M.P.)

Centers for Work Training (C.A.T.)

Homes (Foyers)

nents which are interrelated, all funded under the national plan for handicapped services. First, a center for assisted work (Centre d'aide par le travail; C.A.T.) serves thirty-five adults from 9:00 a.m. to 5:00 p.m. weekdays. Second, thirty-two of these workers live in four group homes which are active from 5:00 p.m. to 9:00 a.m. and on the weekends. Third, a small unit for twelve people with more severe difficulties, called foyer de vie or "home for living," functions twenty-four hours a day. Its residents very often take part in activities with the others in the C.A.T. or group homes.

The finances of La Pradelle are quite complicated, as the components are funded through four separate budgets. The C.A.T. is supported by the national government, while the group homes for workers, and the home for living are supported by the Consul General of the region. A commercial budget results from the products which are sold, including vegetables, fruit, bread, pastries, sausages, and from the proceeds of the guest rooms and restaurant. The fourth budget is the residents' salaries.

The government pays 100 percent of operating expenses, this year 7.5 million francs ($1.5 million) for personnel and 2.5 million ($507,000) for program operations. Additional private contributions are for special purchases such as equipment, vans, or "extras" like holiday expenses.

The daily cost of services at La Pradelle is 640 francs ($130.00) for each worker of the C.A.T. and 590 francs ($120.00) for the residents of the homes for living.

Each public budget must be calculated yearly, and then reviewed by the appropriate administrative agency. It is then either accepted or reduced. As President of the Association, Mme. Grémy's concern is, naturally, that reimbursement will not continue to keep up with inflation or program expenses:

> . . . we fear they will be reduced, or at best not increased for economical governmental reasons. They increased 2% this year while inflation in France was 3.1%. This is worrying.

The government suggests that to make up the difference, or a budget deficit, La Pradelle spend the profits it earns from the work projects.

Mme Grémy: So they told us, "Since you are making profits, you take from the profits." So, you take and diminish it. That is a rather perverse way of thinking, because we might go one year or two years perhaps, but if it goes on like that, it will make . . . pressure on the handicapped people to become productive.

Interviewer: They want you to make up the difference from your commercial profits.

Mme Grémy: We have several budgets. Budgets of the salaries of the staff as a functioning of the C.A.T.; budget of the housing which is provided by the department, the Consul General; budget of the incomes of the handicapped people; and the fourth budget, which is our commercial budget, which is what we sell to the customers, our restaurant, the bread, the pastries. And it is from that budget that we slightly, not very much, but we make some money.

Interviewer: What have you been doing with it so far?

Mme Grémy: So far, we have reemployed it in investments, in equipment . . .

Interviewer: Back into the business.

Mme Grémy: Yes, reinvested it back into the business. We also employed it for the benefit for our residents for holidays and things like that. So if we have to take more of that, it will, of course, be bad for the residents since there will be pressure to be commercial. To be really commercial.

Interviewer: To be there in order to earn money, which really isn't the reason they are there. You are there in order to provide them opportunities. That is an interesting issue regarding revenue from selling products or services. Certain countries are not allowed to sell if they have state monies coming in. So they produce in farmsteads in Holland and Spain, but they cannot sell and earn money that way. We can in the U.S., and we have to figure out how to do that more effectively.

Mme Grémy: And I think that is nice to be able to do that. When the residents of La Pradelle go off to market and sell all their own production, it is good for them. It is not only good for the pocket money . . .

Interviewer: It feels good and they like it and they get rewards . . . Well, La Pradelle is not Club Med and it is not a sweat shop.

Mme Grémy: First, it is place for work and for people who earn their money by working. So they have no choice in the morning, to get up. They must get up to go to work . . .

Interviewer: Do you find very much resistance?

Mme Grémy: Not really, I have not heard about any. It is not, at least, not one of the problems my directors speak about.

Interviewer: I think what happens is that you can take people who like order, and replace their choice of order with what you have awakened them to; your choice of order. And they get just as committed to following the day's schedule in this new life as they were doing meaningless things in the old life. It becomes a ritual in some ways, to get up and go to work . . . like we have rituals.

Mme Grémy: I think also that they have a rather interesting life . . . They have a weekly meeting with their educator where they can discuss the conditions of work, and so if they are not pleased with something they can say it. And even the ones who don't speak have sometimes quiet means of showing if they disagree with something.

This kind of potential focus on profit earning would be contrary to the basic intentions of La Pradelle. Adults with autism are there to partake in the work activities and to learn through them, although as Mme. Grémy points out:

> The fact of having a real salary is very important for the residents who are more considered "workers" than handicapped people. It may appear utopian, but they are really very much interested in managing their money, even those who have severe difficulties.

The salary of the workers in the C.A.T. is 80 percent of the minimum wage in France, but from that one must return payment for his or her food and lodging. Each adult then is left with 1200 francs - $240 dollars each month for clothing, personal and leisure expenses. Residents of the Foyer de Vie have such severe difficulties that they cannot be considered "workers," so they receive an allowance from the government. After they have paid for food and lodging, they have $60 remaining, which she tells us:

> is very little if there is no family to help. In that case, we provide $40 more, monthly, taken from the commercial budget of the C.A.T.

Setting

La Pradelle is located in a rural setting in a valley ringed by low mountains in southern France. Its main house is situated on about 150 acres of hills and arable land. This large house—the C.A.T.—contains a restaurant, guest rooms and a workshop. The six group homes are several miles away.

Residents

Residents at La Pradelle range in age from eighteen to thirty-eight. They represent all forms of autism as well as some cases of adult psychosis. There is a wide range of impairment among the group, with all having serious problems. Madame continues:

We have a very wide range because we don't think to put together high functioning or low functioning would work. If you
put together low functioning people you can put them in lux-
ury, but you will create another psychiatric hospital . . .
   We think that the notion of profit, which we cannot avoid,
must be applied to the whole, but not to one person in particular. So for that [too] we need to have a wide range of levels
of ability.

   To gain admission, parents must apply to a Board of
Examiners called C.O.T.O.R.E.P. La Pradelle is free to accept
or reject candidates once they have been through the
C.O.T.O.R.E.P. assessment. The program is not viable for
those with serious physical deficiencies, but otherwise, het-
erogeneity in the population is considered important. There
is a waiting list of more than 100 families.

Staff

   The employment of trained staff is important at La
Pradelle as it leads to higher levels of competence with less
frequent turnover. Required training for the care workers at
La Pradelle is the three-year college course at one of
France's several schools for educators (École pour d'educa-
teurs). Those employed as monitors have attended an advanced two-year program and receive less pay. There is also
specialized professional training for staff of the various
C.A.T. workshops. On average the ratio of staff to workers is
1:4 during day and early evenings, 1:8 at night, and 1:6 on
weekends.
   The staff consists of the Director who prepares and im-
plements the budgets, manages the professionals and non-
professionals, and coordinates the three centers. He is
assisted by one department head who supervises the workshops, and another who is in charge of the educational programs in the group homes. Two part-time psychiatrists
consult for twenty hours a week on medical issues, and pre-
side at staff meetings, and at meetings with residents.
There are ten monitors for workshops and twenty-two monitors for educational training in the group homes, as well as
four housekeepers, one maintenance worker, one secretary,
and one accountant.

Five family-style homes are in Saumane and l'Est-rechure. Seven to ten residents live in each with the supervision of technical personnel. Residents maintain their own living units and spend their spare time as they choose. The weekly meetings held with the residents are a time for all to speak openly—the educators, workers and boarders all can have their turn as the group attempts to deal with any problems that have arisen. The psychiatrist helps facilitate these exchanges at the meeting in each home, which is anticipated by all and considered essential to that kind of institutional life (Bourdely, p. 2).

Program

Living, working and learning are intentionally integrated throughout this French farm environment. The community at La Pradelle is organized around the work projects which offer the context for social exchanges, communication and communal rules. Daily schedules for La Pradelle's residents vary widely because of the distinct demands of the different work assignments. Those who bake bread begin work at 2 a.m. and work until noon, while those in the restaurant, responsible for serving dinner, stay on until midnight. Care staff remain in each house to maintain as normal a home life as possible for the residents around these different schedules.

A typical day might be scheduled as follows:

7:30 a.m. Get up
          Breakfast
          Dress for the day
9:00 a.m. Leave in the home's minivan to work at the C.A.T.
12:00   Ride home
          Eat lunch which has been prepared in the C.A.T.
2:00 p.m. Return to work
5:00 p.m. Home again in the minivan
          Go shopping with group home family
          Prepare dinner
          Eat
          Decide on evening activity

Workers usually become "rather professional" at their jobs, and often remain at the same assignment for some time. Some may change jobs after a few months. At any one time five or six might be working with the baker, another five or six with the butcher, and several might be assigned to the farmer. The restaurant, run by a cook and assistant cook, employs the three most able residents, while the Inn employs two who can carry out the simpler tasks of changing beds and serving continental breakfast each morning.

Those in the home for living spend their time outdoors caring for vegetable gardens and poultry under supervision of the farmer and an educator.

Products from La Pradelle are in great demand, and are sold in several places. They supply the local grocery store with bread for the village of Saumane, and sell their sausage at a co-op that they share with other farmers. Each Tuesday, in the small nearby town of St. Jean du Gard they rent a stall at the out-door market to sell products, while many customers go directly to the C.A.T. to make their purchases.

In spite of their best plans for the community, the administrators are aware that some areas need continued, even increased, attention. Everyone does not always contribute or share at group meetings, and some staff naturally succumb to the temptation of doing the work in place of the residents. But Monsieur Bourdely believes that despite such issues, the exacting demands made daily of these young adults with autism (or psychosis) permit them some "extension of their own discourse and some relief in living with their problems of existence" (p. 3).

The skill training at La Pradelle is emphasized to help remediate cognitive, social, and communication deficits which are so characteristic of a developmental disability like autism. Medication is used cautiously with efforts made to limit and then diminish the dosage of that which is prescribed. When medicine is prescribed, the matter is discussed between the psychiatrist and the patient, and an explanation is always given before a course of medication is begun. The guiding belief is that a positive environment and a schedule enriched with appropriate work and activity can improve daily life, and may help with the deficiencies and difficulties of the residents. Mme. Grémy is adamant:

> We discard completely, for ethical reasons, the use of aversive techniques implying pain or discomfort, even in situations of aggressivity or self-abuse. Though it is long and difficult, we believe there are other means.

It should be noted that the controversy over the use of aversive techniques with severe developmental disabilities rages on elsewhere (See Gerhardt, Holmes, Alessandri, & Goodman, 1991; Meinhold & Mulick, 1992).

Mme Grémy: And so we say our children need everything that is good for them . . . We want to remain open to all approaches provided, and that is very important. Provided they respect the person of the parent and of the child. And this morning, I have had a lot of arguments with regard to other treatments.

Interviewer: Aversive?

Mme Grémy: Aversive treatments of behavioral problems. I asked one professional when he came to La Pradelle, "What do you do in the case of self-abuse?" I think that is the most difficult thing to change and to be with for parents. I mean, it is dreadful. He told me, "We use modification of behavior." "Ok," I said, "What kind? Do you use aggressive ones?" "No, very rarely." I said, "What is very rarely? Do you mean two or three percent of the cases?" "For instance, if someone bangs his head, we put in the electric hat. When he bangs his head he gets electric shock." My director, Bourdeley was there, he said, "I cannot; even for one percent." "If you accept it for one percent. . ."

Interviewer: That's what is done in some places.

Mme Grémy: I said, "That I cannot accept." If you accept the principle that it might be one percent for you, for another one it might be two, three, five, ten, there is no limit. I think there are other means. I think of what happened at La Pradelle. I'm thinking of one man who arrived, he was bald on one part of his head because he always banged the same part. He had his hands completely sore from biting and so on. We didn't put him in an electric hat, needless to say. I think that having him in an interesting setting, exposing him to interesting things to do, we have not cured that in four days. I was told it took four days to get them to stop banging their head with an electric hat. It took about eight or ten months here, and sometimes still happens when he rests. It's not gone, but his hair is quite nice now. His hands also. So I think there are other ways. Our policy is to still remain open to everything, provided we avoid that; because, I will never accept that. Never and from what I have read from your book . . .

Interviewer: We don't do that at Bittersweet Farms and we have had people who had hurt themselves. Not so bad but . . .

Mme Grémy: Then there was the boy who tore his clothes. "Buy him clothes that can't be torn," they said. But first they are difficult to find. Terrible. What would you do? He was very strong. I think he could bend steel, you know. And to me, it is not a solution. But what have the staff done? He earns money. The staff told him, because then the institution could not pay for the clothes. We had to ask the parents and they bought. And they bought about two thousand francs a month the amount of clothes. So that staff told the boy that it was not possible; but it was going on. "Your parents cannot pay two thousand francs a month, and we cannot, the institution cannot afford that. What we are going to do is we are going to buy clothes with you." We went to buy clothes with him and he is paying for his clothes, and slowly and slowly he continued for awhile . . .

Interviewer: His money, his money . . .

Mme Grémy: When his money was out, "Well," we said. "You can't have more money; you have spent it in clothes." And now he feels it's almost finished.

Interviewer: I believe that you are right. I think that you can find such a behavioral approach.

Mme Grémy: I suppose so, but the kind of behavioral I like.

Interviewer: We had a boy who tore his clothes and they came to the conclusion that what he liked was new clothes. So they bought him a wardrobe of all the same clothes. Same overalls and same T-shirts. So when he had to change his clothes, it was not better for him; it was the same thing. That was one piece of the program. The problem was repaired over time with these kinds of behavioral maneuvers. In a similar situation, they gave another young man something else that he could tear at a certain time of the day. He could just tear, and tear, and tear and be done. But they did not make a reward out of tearing. The use of aversive stimuli is very controversial in the United States, too.

Leisure

Staff-resident relationships are on-going and continuous, as they extend from work to meals to recreational activities. Therefore, social and communicative skills (among others) learned in one setting can be applied elsewhere and integrated more fully by the residents.

Activities beyond work are also considered important at La Pradelle, for during their spare time the residents can relate to neighbors in the town and expand their range of human exchanges. Some sing in a choir in the nearby village, while several women exercise in the local gym. Each group's home has its own budget, so with help from the staff everyone shops for food for their breakfast and evening meals, and makes personal purchases from earned income. Management of one's personal money is guided by an educator and allows for individual spending as a natural consequence or outcome of work completed.

There are recreational and sports activities during free time and on the weekends. Residents go out to restaurants or to the cinema. Different leisure and recreation options are chosen by each group home. Choices include hiking, biking, horseback riding, canoeing, climbing, and water skiing. There is also an on-going theatre workshop within the La Pradelle community.

Community relationships and farmstead-community interchanges are by no means unidirectional. Neighbors come to La Pradelle's restaurant and guest rooms to buy the breads, pastries, and salamis made there. At times visitors attend special dinners presented with an accompanying jazz group or singers.

Family involvement and visiting schedules are varied and depend on agreements made between each resident, his or her family, and the staff. Visits to families may be scheduled every two weeks, once a month, or every two months. Families can meet with staff whenever they wish, and the staff may ask a family to come to La Pradelle if there is an issue that needs to be discussed.

Summer is the busiest season for the activities at La Pradelle, so all the residents earn six weeks of vacation each year and generally enjoy it when the busy tourist season ends. If they don't go off with their families, they might travel with a La Pradelle group camping or staying at a beach-side house. They have even vacationed in Spain. Typically, six or seven residents will be accompanied by two staff. They might leave for a three-week trip to the mountains or sea-side which is funded through private donations.

Forward Look

We can use the farmstead model of La Pradelle as one example of the developmental history of this genre of residential treatment environments. As with most farms, it was initiated and organized by concerned parent and professional groups which formed links with governmental and private resource bases. Charismatic, highly intelligent, and powerful individuals made the "farmsteads" happen, and then with the assistance of other parents, volunteers, and nonprofessional staff the centers provide full-fledged education and treatment. We see this process: 1) Once begun and operating, the farms come under closer scrutiny and end up with professional administration and an even more "professionalized" staff. Objectives then focus on evaluation of program effectiveness, costs, educational and treatment options—a new era of leadership and management. 2) The idiosyncrasy and uniqueness of each farm may diminish as the new era begins. Farmstead philosophers and practitioners visit each other and change each other; they move toward a common and widely accepted set of propositions about staff, residents, programs, and so on. The generic farmstead community is born and with it the opportunity to become more global, cost-effective and reproducible, yet at the same time to retain the shape and coloration of each country and region. 3) As the ontogeny of each farmstead occurs, the intervention approaches suggested in Smith's (1990) book "Autism and Life in the Community" will become salient for many professional staff. Behavioral assessment and functional analysis of problematic behaviors of a resident will be more carefully performed. Specific intervention plans will be written, used, and revised. The conception of behavior as sets of "skills" is useful, since that speaks to observable and teachable or trainable behaviors, and an optimistic view of autism in adulthood. In particular, social, vocational, and communication skills training can be originated which suits different farmsteads and the varying levels of functioning of adult residents. 4) It is not overly optimistic, too, to imagine that the training of residents will be conceptualized in ways that go beyond improving "skills" or modifying "behaviors." Even now, more is obviously occurring within the minds of farmstead residents than is easily recognized or clearly seen in behavior; this unnoticed activity has to do with thinking and remembering, as well as other aspects of cognitive function.

The work of Powell and Jordan (1992) sets forth twelve principles for teaching problem-solving to adults with autism within their so-called "cognitive curriculum." Two of their major areas are called "creating a thinking environment" and "enabling learning through social and emotional routes." In the first area, the authors stress the need to establish a relationship of mutual trust and acceptance with a resident, a non-threatening environment which values feedback and experimentation, and a practice that residents take as much responsibility for their own learning as possible. In the second area, they are concerned with using a resident's interests as a vehicle to make tasks have meaning and relevance for these individuals. Residents need to use their emotions and self-awareness of emotional states, to enhance their memory; teachers need to make meanings explicit or else attribute meaning to a resident's contribution; and teachers should, especially, attune the rhythm and speed of the learning environment to the adult with autism, so that their participation is encouraged.

Mme. Grémy and the other leaders of Languedoc-Roussillon and La Pradelle have a dramatic and ambitious vision for the future that encompasses emotional, structural, and pragmatic realms. There are plans to do more work with families in the future, to help them make the transition from dealing with their offspring as children to relating to them as adolescents and then adults.

Because the location of La Pradelle is still somewhat remote, a new home is being purchased closer to the local community with hopes of facilitating a more natural integration into the local activities. Mme. Grémy actually envisions several small communities being built, so that workers might have the option of moving from time to time to a setting with different homes and different work projects. Such a network could provide a continuing rotation of people offering new experiences and new learning, and introducing "more dynamism." Looking ahead, she says:

> I think we know that they need protection all their lives. I mean, it is silly to think that they will be voting one day and going for employment just as everyone. That is just a dream. A big dream.

However, for those workers who become more self-sufficient in their jobs, there are currently placements in the community for trial periods in shops and hotels. More of that is planned.

Sésame-Autism Languedoc-Roussillon is now planning a large new project. It is described as a "Holiday Recreation and Cultural Center for both able and disabled individuals, with or without their families." It is to be a resort managed under the French system of services for disabled people. This would be a vacation setting in southern France, near Marseilles, that would offer water and equestrian activities. It would be a place where those with autism, especially those trained in the workshops, restaurant, and Inn at La Pradelle, could be employed. They would work alongside professional staff and have available any assistance they might need. In turn, the resort hopes to be available "to a broad spectrum of vacationers including able bodied people and those accompanied by persons with very different types of handicaps (physical, mental, sensorial, or chronic illness)."

There is hope for future additional staff at La Pradelle to allow for more individualized attention for the residents and to permit more systematic record keeping and documentation of each resident's progress in all areas of development. Currently, there are no government mandates for record keeping and little staff time available for such efforts. Every three months a comprehensive report is completed for each resident. When more continuous assessments can be made, there might be a way to study the changes that take place through the experience of living and working at La Pradelle.

Optimism is generated by Etienne Daum's (Autism Europe Association, 1992) summary of meetings between parent associations and professionals in France:

> . . . the climate appears quite favorable and concrete proposals could result—for example, a more favorable system for financing establishments which cater for people with autism; additional training for professionals who work with them, and above all, support for innovating initiatives in the area of educational care as an alternative to the present set-up (p. 11).

To conclude, we feel certain that the original and creative vision of La Pradelle will prevail. There is a degree of political influence in the hands of the regional association, but the battle to increase funding from government and local authorities, to improve staff ratio, remains difficult. The ability to raise private funds for vans and equipment is impressive. But much remains to be done. Changes are needed in the training of psychiatrists and educators in areas where psychoanalysis still maintains great influence. The use of behavioral techniques requires that staff have the time and expertise available for data collection, the establishment of baselines for each individual resident, and the development of intervention strategies. More staff are needed also in order to reach the accepted levels of the most successful and established farmsteads elsewhere, and to avoid inordinate degrees of staff stress and eventual, but unnecessary, burn-out.

Dr. Leo Kannerhuis
Oosterbeek, Holland

There is no better illustration of the need for individualized programming than the gradual evolution leading to Wolfheze, Holland's workhome and farm program for adults with autism. The scope of the Dr. Leo Kannerhuis philosophy and program will be described as a prelude, for it is out of that experience that Wolfheze was born.

The Dr. Leo Kannerhuis is the name of Holland's only facility specifically devoted to the residential treatment of adolescents and adults with autism. It is highly professionalized and clearly exemplifies the principles of program individualization, structure in living and learning settings, and carefully thought out and planned skills training.

The Intermural Health Services of the Netherlands provides 4.5 percent of the country's total social care budget, and the most generously funded service within that designation is residential youth psychiatry. Dr. Leo Kannerhuis, considered a residential youth psychiatric service, was opened in 1974 in the affluent town of Oosterbeek in central Holland.

Origins

The program began in the early 1970's when Mr. Auping, a parent of a child with autism, donated money to create the first home. He chose Professor Kamp from Utrecht and Professor Dumont from Nijmegen University to provide professional support, and together they created a foundation in Oosterbeek called Help for Autistic Children and Adolescents (Stichting Hulp aan Autistische Kinderen en Adolescenten, SHAKA). Mr. Anton Hoogveld, an orthopedagogue and private teacher of Auping's son, was chosen to be the first director. Set in a picturesque, wealthy suburban neighborhood, the Dr. Leo Kannerhuis thus began as home and training site for eight adolescents with autism.

Today, in 1992, the program has grown to occupy five neighborhood homes in Oosterbeek, two houses in a village nearby, and four family homes in its rural long-stay center on the grounds of a psychiatric facility at Wolfheze. Each home accommodates five or six residents and attending staff. There are currently sixty-two residents in the Kannerhuis programs supported by a staff of 125. Administrative offices are located in the "mother-house" in Oosterbeek, a recently renovated large home with well-appointed offices and conference rooms.

The average cost for daily care at Kannerhuis is $250. Costs for all care and training are paid by the Dutch government, for exceptional medical expenses are part of the national insurance scheme. The medical insurance law decrees that until age eighteen parents' insurance covers all costs. After age eighteen the state pays 250 Guilders a month ($1,256.68) plus payment for the client's own insurance. If some money is earned by a client in a sheltered workshop, adjustments are made resulting in a monthly income of 1200 Guilders each month ($752.04).

At age twenty-three a client receives a monthly wage of 2000 Guilders ($1,253.40) plus his payment to insurance. Any patient who earns more than 50,000 Guilders ($31,335) must cover his own insurance's short-term costs, but long-term costs are still paid by the state. The government does not permit people in residential settings like Leo Kannerhuis to earn additional money through sale of the products they make or grow there.

Residents

High-functioning adolescents with autism are sent to Kannerhuis from all regions of Holland to enter an orthopsychological treatment program that focuses primarily on the teaching of social skills and communication. Those with IQ levels below the normal range continue to be grouped in large and small institutions throughout Holland in programs for those with mental retardation.

Residents of Kannerhuis range in age from fourteen to twenty-one. Criteria for admission include a diagnosis of autism, absence of severe mental handicap as shown by psychological assessment, understanding of language with at least minimal verbal expression, and the need for a residential setting. Scores in the area of social intelligence must range between 80 and 140 on the Wechsler Intelligence Scale for Children. Indications of a wide discrepancy between verbal and performance scores—a "disharmonic profile"—are typical of this group according to van Belle-Bakker (1992).

Staff: We do not focus on one intelligence quotient. We focus on this harmonic profile. There is a boy in G which we will meet this afternoon. He has a performance quotient of 140. He has a verbal quotient of 100, so it's average and he has a social quotient of 90 which is not too bad. Well, this profile is so disharmonic that we say he is, in the first place, very autistic. He is a real autistic person. The higher functioning pupils show many more depressive states and in some cases even get suicidal just because of the higher functioning.

Interviewer: They understand their condition?

Staff: Yes, and they come and when they don't have the opportunity and the means to change, then it's a very hard time for them.

Interviewer: So they need all the support they can get. Then that's what makes the difference.

Staff: Yes, and it's rather strange to see that even those high figures, like this boy, well, he might be one who gets to go to the lower technical school; but then he's one of the exceptions. Most of them, even at those higher figures, just are at their maximum when they can work in a sheltered workshop.

Candidates must be able to maneuver within a traditional suburban home that is not handicap accessible. Those residents who are accepted are expected to stay in residence about three years, although some remain for five. Of the forty-two residents in seven homes, there are thirty-three males and nine females.

In recent years in Holland, more early schooling and community services have become available for children and adolescents with autism, so the referral pool for Kannerhuis has begun to include more difficult-to-manage residents. To meet this need, the program has created two environments with more intensive staff support. The house called Zip, a Dutch acronym for "very intensive treatment," has four residents and allows two additional spaces for residents from other houses who might be in crisis and need respite from their regular treatment regimen. There is a full-time equivalent staff of six at Zip to mange these more challenging situations.

Parents

The search for the right diagnosis and treatment has long been a problem for parents of young children with autism in Holland. To illustrate one path, we cite the early education of a fifteen-year-old boy currently at Kannerhuis which began when he was five. He first attended a school for the deaf at Arnhem where he was enrolled in speech therapy. He then attended a pedagogical institute in the town of Nijmegen that served children with minimal brain dysfunction and dyslexia. He began there at age seven and was able to stay there all day including an after-school program held in a home on the grounds until 5:30 p.m. At age twelve, this young man was enrolled at Kannerhuis, while he still attended school one day a week in Nijmegen where he studied reading, cooking, household tasks, self-care and social skills among children with mental retardation. He could read well and do arithmetic. His parents expect him to remain at Kannerhuis for a total of five years and have seen important changes in his social skills since he began there.

Interviewer: Now he's been here 2 ½ years, have you seen any changes?

Father: Oh, yes.

Interviewer: What do you see has changed in 2 ½ years?

Mother: Now when we are going to other people, we can take him with us. So he is sitting in a chair and looking at the telephone.

Interviewer: He didn't used to be able to do that?

Mother: Oh no! He was always walking and jumping and very . . .

Interviewer: . . . active and distracted?

Mother: . . . yes, yes. When you went home he was very tired, and now he's gorgeous, he's sitting and very quiet.

Father: He is the best behaving child of our three children. (laughs) We can take him out easily, we can take him to a restaurant or to friends or to . . .

Mother: Yes, and when he was younger, it was a disaster.

Interviewer: Uh-huh, so that's a change. What are some problems that you still would like to see changed?

Mother: He can't go alone on the street. He doesn't watch if there is a car, and that's a pity, so he can't go alone to the shop, and that sort of thing. And he doesn't like to be alone home, so you always take him with you if you go shopping for ten minutes, that sort of thing.

Father: That's what he also likes to do. So that's not only a matter of, that he does not want to stay at home, but he wants to come with you. He used to chew on his thumb very much, and that's what we said also, "Can you stop that?" I think they managed that quite well.

Staff

The nature of the staff and their roles and activities deserve careful consideration and study here. To serve and support the sixty-two residents in all of its programs, Kannerhuis provides 125.3 full time equivalent staff positions. For the most part, a ratio of one staff to two residents is maintained, with a full complement of professional, nonprofessional, and support staff.

A varied assortment of mental health staff are present. Professional staff includes a psychiatrist who provides diagnoses as well as advice and treatment of related psychiatric disorders or symptoms. A psychologist works part-time providing diagnostic assessments, professional advice, and research expertise. Orthopedagogues, equivalent to child psychologists, are responsible for client treatment. They provide written training programs for the residents and supervise the staff who carry out the programs. The orthodidactic is responsible for cognitive assessments and designs school programs. One speech therapist diagnoses and provides therapy for speech and language disorders, focusing primarily on semantic and pragmatic difficulties.

There are three social workers who are involved with intake, support and advice for parents. They seek residential home and sheltered workshop placements and services for those who move on from Kannerhuis.

Additional staff and therapists include the following: One physio-therapist runs weekly group sessions and offers individual diagnosis and treatment when needed. A music therapist holds weekly group sessions and individual therapy. And a treatment manager has overall responsibility for all treatment programs, management of personnel, and treatment policy. There is a physician available in the town when someone is ill, and medical specialists including a neurologist are available when needed. All residents visit a dentist regularly.

Staff within each house are specially trained social pedagogues and orthodidactics who have had three years of study in residential training, allowing them to develop expertise in such areas as stimulating group dynamics, carrying out behavioral programs, or more generally working with those with emotional or developmental handicaps.

When they are employed at the Dr. Leo Kannerhuis, they are given three days of in-service training on implementing skill programs and later attend regular study days on various related topics. A team leader and an orthopedagogue supervise all staff members.

There is one male and one female staff member assigned to each shift in each house. Evening staff who sleep from 11:00 p.m. to 7:00 a.m. arrive at 3:00 p.m. and remain until 3:00 p.m. of the following day, overlapping day and evening shifts and providing continuity for residents. Many of the house staff are content to work thirty-six or twenty-four hour weeks as they are well compensated for the work they do. The average per diem cost for residents at Dr. Leo Kannerhuis is about $250, and 70 percent of that earned budget goes to pay staff salaries.

In addition to professional staff, there are housekeepers who do the daily cleaning in each home and provide laundry service; cooks prepare meals in a large common kitchen for distribution to each house. Gardeners groom the shrubs and lawns, maintaining the grounds in accord with neighborhood standards. During alternate weekends when they are not visiting their parents, more of the professional housekeeping chores are assumed by the residents.

Treatment Program

The philosophy at Kannerhuis holds that residents can learn and adjust best when grouped with others at a similar functional level. The living unit is the center of treatment for them. Grouped homogeneously, residents live and receive treatment with others at a corresponding verbal and social level. These range from units A and B where behaviors are most ritualistic and bizarre, to units E and F where pupils are highly verbal and able to interact within a structured social setting. For those with the most severe autistic disturbances, treatment is often carried out on an individual basis while optimal structure and predictability are maintained. If more socially attuned, their treatment is facilitated in group sessions with focus on improvement of social and practical skills. Efforts are made to prepare this group for school or job settings after their discharge from Kannerhuis.

The treatment team in each living unit is composed of four or five group leaders, a group head, a social worker, and a remedial teacher according to Berger (p.9). Each pupil has a mentor, one of the group leaders in the house, who acts as confidante and practical assistant offering personal support when needed. Details of specific daily treatment programs are developed for each pupil during monthly pupil-oriented team meetings attended by the remedial teacher, psychiatrist, social worker, group head, and group leader.

Twice a year the pupil's progress is discussed with parents in the presence of the social worker, mentor, and remedial teacher. There is an annual plenary discussion during which the mentor's written observation report is discussed with the entire multidisciplinary team. Here the psychiatrist, psychologist, coordinating head of therapy, remedial teacher, speech therapist, kinesiotherapists, and physiotherapists as well as job trainers, all gather to establish treatment goals, specific treatment approaches and a time frame for realization of the plan.

Parents can contribute to this plenary meeting as well. More generally, too, parent involvement is important at Kannerhuis. Most pupils regularly visit their parents at home, while parents come to visit at Kannerhuis on alternating weekends.

Treatment Method

The program is committed to promoting a comprehensive set of life skills. In their document *Treatment in The Dr. Leo Kannerhuis* (Berger, 1991), the staff describe their training methods in great detail. The following draws upon information from that document. They are concerned most with developing skills which will enhance future life and work for their adolescents and young adults with autism. These target areas are:

- social and emotional development
- development of language and communication
- development of practical skills
- development of professional and working skills
- cognitive development
- development of leisure time activities
- physical, sensory-motor development

Each skill area is taught through programs developed at the Dr. Leo Kannerhuis. The particular emphasis of teaching for each pupil is determined once their needs have been assessed through supplementary testing, and staff members have gotten a sense of their growth potential. Care is taken neither to understimulate nor to overly challenge each pupil, and once skills are learned in remedial situations they are practiced and generalized to different contexts.

For the most important area of social and emotional development, Kannerhuis describes the focus of specific skills taught:

- Social interactions: introducing oneself, saying hello, please and thank-you, receiving visitors.
- Establishing contact: making eye contact, initiating a conversation, asking for help, demonstrating a willingness to help.
- Reacting to someone else's initiative to make contact: listening, maintaining a topic, taking turns, answering questions.
- Cooperating with others: Stating one's own opinion, discussing, making choices, reaching compromises, making subtle distinctions in criticism.
- Having fun with others: romping about, playing games, sharing hobbies.
- Recognizing emotions: happiness, cheerfulness, sadness, and anger.

Exercises are prescribed for each of these skill areas and ultimately "the pupils are kept alert all the time: practice continues during meals, coffee and tea breaks, group discussions and group meetings, sport, play and manual skills," according to Berger (p.12).

Targeted during communication and language training are all "autistic characteristics in language use." These include goals to reduce "echolalia, neologisms, absolute statements and inversions of personal pronouns." Beyond speech therapy sessions and throughout the day, feedback is given regarding these autistic characteristics, as well as additional issues like rate of speech, intonation patterns, and loudness levels. Grammar is attended to as well within the more general pragmatic skill of passing information on to others in an "ordered and understandable way."

Practical skills taught systematically include personal hygiene, shopping for food and clothing, simple cooking, and some independent travel. Money management training is offered to those who have the potential to understand it. Those most able at Kannerhuis are given professional and work skill training to prepare them for the world beyond this treatment setting. Technical training is provided in a workshop, a greenhouse, and a garden. This job training is geared to preparing pupils to work in special sheltered workshops in Holland where they would earn some money for their efforts.

The workshop director provides exquisitely detailed, visually cued programs for all tasks taught. Photo sequences or printed words and diagrams are used as appropriate to the needs and abilities of each pupil. Workshop tasks taught and guided include wood construction, painting projects, and metal work. Residents learn greenhouse skills like preparing soil for planting, planting seeds or cuttings, cultivating, watering, and attending both indoor plants and outdoor gardens and lawns. For those less able, skills usable in an activity center are pursued. More routine tasks are available there like paper-cutting, candle-making, or assembling small items and packaging them.

Cognitive training continues in the education program at Dr. Leo Kannerhuis, where through the special education techniques required, students are taught language, reading, writing, and arithmetic. Measuring, weighing, telling time, and counting money are also included where possible. More practical learning offered involves study of the library, the police station and the government. Some students participate on a part-time basis in their local school program, but this is kept to a minimum so as not to interfere with the Dr. Leo Kannerhuis focus on "the development of life skills."

The residents at Kannerhuis are hardly ever idle. To help their pupils learn how to make use of their free-time, Kannerhuis offers hobby clubs including snacks, drama, model building, games, dance and movement. Leisure activities like reading or playing musical instruments are encouraged and clubs in the outside community are available for those independent enough to take part in them. To advance physical and sensory motor development handwork, training in movement and gymnastics is offered at Kannerhuis, along with games and sports. Each week the pupils go to a nearby sports center for athletic options. All teaching at Dr. Leo Kannerhuis is done methodically and systematically:

> knowledge is transferred in a very structured fashion, extended and varied step by step, continually repeated and tested. (Berger, 1991, p. 14).

For those adolescents and young adults whose visual-spatial intelligence is within the normal range, visual aids including video taped examples are used frequently. Behavior is modeled by others and role playing is incorporated.

> The pupils learn to analyse tasks using check-lists and flow diagrams, to apply their newly acquired knowledge in practice by means of homework, and to reflect on their own behavior using record forms which they fill in themselves. (Berger, 1991, p. 14).

Pupils at all skill levels learn to talk about their own behaviors and discuss the behaviors of others as well. Staff and residents at Kannerhuis have developed their own colloquial vocabulary. When referring to personal obsessions or preoccupations, so common to this population, they call them "fips." It seems to be a term that with less formality allows for some levity and humor as the topic is discussed, yet insures a consensual understanding.

Throughout all the teaching that goes on at the Dr. Leo Kannerhuis, efforts are made to make the residents truly feel at home, while at the same time gently and continuously challenging them to perform at their highest level. Staff members must have a tolerance for the idiosyncrasies of the autistic disorder combined with the behavior modification skills to teach and consistently reward more appropriate behaviors. Berger goes on to say:

> If there is too much tolerance, there is a danger that development will stagnate. But greater danger accompanies too great a remedial force: then the pupil may well lose his personal equilibrium and disintegrate. The treatment is only ethically sound when one finds the proper balance. (p. 11).

TYPICAL WEEK AT DR. LEO KANNERHUIS

Monday:

09.00 - 10.00	Small jobs in the house
10.30 - 12.00	Job training greenhouse/garden
13.30 - 15.00	Group program Problem Solving Skills
15.30 - 17.00	Baking (cookies, cake etc.) in the ward
19.15 - 21.15	Sewing lesson (outdoors)

Tuesday

09.00 - 12.00	Group program Training Social Skills
13.30 - 15.00	Leisure time
15.30 - 17.00	Job training workshop
18.30 - 21.00	Sports (in a sport accomodation with various groups of the Leo Kannerhuis)

Wednesday

09.00 - 10.30	Creative activities
11.00 - 12.00	Language
14.00 - 15.00	Weekly talk with personal group-leader (mentor)
15.30 - 17.00	Bank/shopping
19.30 - 20.30	Ward meeting

Thursday

09.00 - 10.00	Self-managing/self-care
10.30 - 12.00	Swimming (with the group)
13.30 - 15.00	Leisure time
15.45 - 17.00	Sports (in a sports hall in a school nearby)
19.00 - 20.00	Clubs (in the house, like cooking, creative, drama, etc.)

Friday

09.00 - 10.00	Music therapy with the group
10.30 - 12.00	Straightening own room
13.30 - 17.00	Preparation for the weekend/leisure time.

Medication is considered only in cases of multiple tics, excessive restlessness, or when psychotic agitation and aggression is displayed.

The question of what constitutes a success or positive outcome for residential treatment of adolescents with autism is tricky. Recall that for most, adolescent or adult autism is a permanent condition, not reversible, marked by occasional retrogressions, and replete with severe communication, emotional, cognitive, physical, and ritualistic behaviors and symptoms. Bluntly, it would be unreasonable to expect a "cure" to result from residential treatment, or for mature relationships to become a sign of farmstead-fostered social skill development. Progress must be judged in small increments, based on behavior change, consistency, and durability, and be focused on proximal (not distal) variables and on process (not outcome) characteristics. Do education and treatment lead to a more complete and satisfying human existence? Is residential treatment more effective if more and better trained staff and others in a social support system are involved?

Berger (1983) has conducted one of the few controlled studies of the effects of residential treatment on adolescent autism. Using a pretest-posttest design he compared twenty-five inpatients at the Leo Kannerhuis House with twelve adolescents with autism who had not been admitted and lived at home with their parents or in a mental home. Kannerhuis accepts youngsters with autism (severe mental deficiency excluded), so they must reach an IQ of 85 on at least one of a variety of intelligence tests. Social intelligence, for example, is measured by the WAIS, WISC-R, SON Picture Arrangement, or the SIT Test. The integrated "environmental therapy" involves combined, purposive activity during domestic chores, group projects, school, sport, and so on. Briefly, the Leo Kannerhuis students showed significantly more gain in their social intelligence—which indicates more ability in interpersonal behavior, increased capacity to understand other people, and an enhanced self-critical quality. Future studies need to pin down the features of the residential treatment which are associated with change.

Discharge Planning

After providing years of careful treatment, appreciative of the resident's deep-seated vulnerability despite the layers of acquired skills, the staff and administrators of the Dr. Leo Kannerhuis remain heavily invested in placements and future assignments. One administrator describes some concerns regarding workshop settings:

They just don't pick up the routine. They get puzzled by the noise; they get puzzled by the pressure . . . How many things do you have to do? Maybe sometimes they have to learn to change some activity.

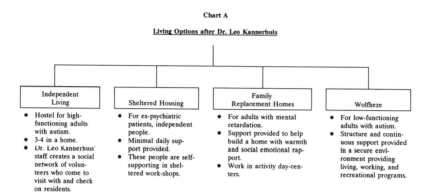

Chart A

Living Options after Dr. Leo Kannerhuis

Independent Living	Sheltered Housing	Family Replacement Homes	Wolfheze
• Hostel for high-functioning adults with autism. • 3-4 in a home. • Dr. Leo Kannerhuis' staff creates a social network of volunteers who come to visit with and check on residents.	• For ex-psychiatric patients, independent people. • Minimal daily support provided. • These people are self-supporting in sheltered work-shops.	• For adults with mental retardation. • Support provided to help build a home with warmth and social emotional rapport. • Work in activity day-centers.	• For low-functioning adults with autism. • Structure and continuous support provided in a secure environment providing living, working, and recreational programs.

Options for more permanent placement must be identified for each pupil after two to five years in treatment at the Dr. Leo Kannerhuis. Choices shown in Chart A include several living and working settings that were originally established for those with mental retardation or psychiatric problems. With careful introduction by staff and very gradual transitions, many graduates of the Kannerhuis program have been accommodated in such settings. However, as the number of pupils increases, and the severity of disorders of the newer groups becomes greater, there is concern that placements will be more difficult to find. Moreover, the government of the Netherlands, as elsewhere, is under increasing financial pressure. There is worry that sheltered workshops will become centers for more potentially productive citizens who remain on the public rolls. Such workshops will be under pressure to produce more goods and earn more money and, as a consequence, may have less use for workers with retardation or autism. If that is the case, then the Dr. Leo Kannerhuis might have to create its own after-care settings.

Currently, there are several residential possibilities. Independent living units are an option for the highest functioning young adults with autism. Three to four individuals live in a neighborhood home and take care of their own daily needs. They may have regular jobs or might work in a sheltered workshop. To provide some continuing social support, the Dr. Leo Kannerhuis staff has created networks of volunteers who stop by, informally, to visit with the residents and to make sure everything is all right.

For those who continue to need minimal daily support, sheltered housing is available. This arrangement was originally created for ex-psychiatric patients, and provides supportive staff who check with residents on a periodic basis. The residents of those homes throughout Holland are self-supporting as they work in sheltered workshops.

Family Replacement Homes were established for adults with mental retardation. Here staff support is provided within the home to help create warmth and social-emotional rapport among the residents. These people spend most of their time in activity day-centers.

Finally, there is the special setting for those who are considered to have a severe form of autism; Wolfheze, established in 1987, provides structure and continuous support in a secure environment within which the residents live, work, and engage in recreational programs. As the population with these needs is recognized and grows, many such settings will be needed. Several programs modeled after Wolfheze are in various stages of development in North, Central, and Southern Holland at this time. There are plans for eventual creation of similar workhouses in each of the Dutch provinces (Demeestere, p. 89).

Wolfheze

The intense and demanding quality of treatment at Kannerhuis was not appropriate for all adolescents with autism. It became clear that something else was needed. On the tenth anniversary of the Dr. Leo Kannerhuis, the Dutch Ministry of Welfare, Housing, and Culture gave permission for the founding of a workhome as an extension of the Kannerhuis program (Kaiser, p. 2).

To plan for this new project, personnel from Dr. Leo Kannerhuis traveled around Europe to gather information from existing residential programs for adults with autism. They visited Le Grand Royal in France, Longford Court, and Somerset Court in England and a small program in Belgium. They saw efforts to incorporate various degrees of behavior modification techniques and observed models that integrated residential, vocational, and leisure programming. They met other directors, each with different attitudes toward their residents or clients and with various degrees of control over the components of their projects. They returned with a sense of the elements they felt would be critical to Wolfheze.

The Wolfheze project opened in 1987 in a rural setting fifteen minutes from Oosterbeek on one and one-half acres of the National Psychiatric Hospital complex. It includes four homes connected by large recreation rooms. Five residents live in each home with two staff members in attendance throughout the day and evening. Here, according to Kaiser (1987), residents over eighteen years of age with "chronic autistic syndrome" are provided a setting in which living, working, and leisure are integrated in a safe and secure environment. Continuity of staff and daily schedules is assured so the residents can enjoy "a kind of life in which they are happy despite their autistic characteristics."

The founders of this program distinguished between the treatment focus at Dr. Leo Kannerhuis and the care and teaching at Wolfheze:

> . . . the difference between a treatment and such a residential ward is that in a treatment ward the atmosphere is put at the service of treatment, that is to say aimed at the improvement of the autistic symptoms. In a residential ward, the treatment is in and of the autists holding their own in this atmosphere, aimed at their being happy. Here special "therapeutic programmes in a narrower sense" will not be applied, but preventing backsliding is the target. (Kaiser, p. 3).

Wolfheze Setting

Wolfheze has been a mixed blessing. It strives to accommodate to the needs of those with more challenging behaviors yet it is somewhat stigmatized by its location. The town of Wolfheze is a fifteen-minute drive from Oosterbeek along scenic country roads, but the town is best known throughout Holland for its state psychiatric facility. The long-term care program created by the Dr. Leo Kannerhuis staff for twenty adults with autism is actually situated on the property of this hospital complex. The grounds are quite spacious and the hospital buildings are spread out on the property, out of view of the workhome compound.

The buildings at Wolfheze are unpretentious. Four narrow modest homes with sharply pointed dormers edge the compound. Each has a small living room, kitchen and dining area on the first floor and a bedroom for each resident upstairs. A large recreation room with its own kitchen connects two of the dwellings and serves as the setting for indoor leisure activities.

Plenty of opportunities for arts, crafts, and horticulture exist. The activities compound lies a short walk from the homes and includes a spacious and well equipped wood working factory where a wide variety of wooden toys are cut, sanded, assembled, and painted. An arts and crafts room with well supplied shelves along the walls contains a big table and enough chairs for groups involved in creative activities. Animals cared for include two small Chinese pigs, some goats, sheep, and chickens. A large greenhouse is used as the work setting for residents involved in the agricultural program. A variety of flower and vegetable plants are prepared here for transplanting into the large gardens each spring. Crops produced are eaten by the community and some are shared with families of residents. Since the Dutch government prohibits the earning of money by subsidized residential facilities, produce cannot be sold to earn money to support the programs or to pay the residents.

Staff at Wolfheze

Here, too, staff are highly trained and once they are on the job, in-service teaching provides them with additional skills relevant to this setting. The twenty residents at Wolfheze are supported in their homes, at work, and at leisure by a staff of twenty-five plus one farmer, one person who runs the wood products factory, and two half-time creative arts teachers. Staff work side by side with residents, and all staff members at Wolfheze get to know all the residents well, so it is easy to interchange staff between the houses and work settings if necessary without disrupting the residents.

Staff members are all trained orthopedagogues who relate to the residents warmly, with support and sensitive understanding of their needs. There are always two staff members in attendance during waking hours for each home, and one who sleeps on the premises.

Record keeping at Wolfheze entails daily notes written about each resident. If any unusual problems arise, they are carefully described and solutions are implemented. The notes written by the staff members in each house are read and evaluated by the director.

Residents

The twenty residents of Wolfheze are now between twenty-three and thirty-six years of age. Most were originally in treatment at Dr. Leo Kannerhuis, but reacted negatively to the demands of the program, the degree of change in daily schedules, or the amount of flexibility encouraged there. Some would react with tantrums; others withdrew. It was obvious to the staff that their needs were not being met and that they did not have the capacity to integrate the changes required to move on to less-structured sheltered group homes or workshop settings.

Their assignment to Wolfheze is considered placement for the rest of their lives. In this comfortable home environment, treatment protocols to reduce autistic symptoms have been removed and exchanged for learning through doing in partnership with attending staff. Only in cases where behaviors become dangerous or destructive are "treatment" programs established. Parents are encouraged to gradually distance themselves from their now adult children, explains a staff member:

We think it is a big task . . . for the social workers. They have to go to talk with the parents. Some parents can stand it very well, and they have gone their own way, and some parents— they keep a hold of their children. The way the work home is arranged—as a small world of its own . . . everybody can see what is going on, everybody knows the rules and what is the structure and what is the program, where they live, and they can see how it is working out; parents don't disturb in a world they do not understand. I think that is the way of organizing such a project for autistic people.

Wolfheze Supported Learning

Activities at Wolfheze proceed at a more relaxed pace in contrast to the fully packed Kannerhuis treatment program. Schedules are set so each resident knows what is to be done each week. One week of each month is for housework, one for wood shop, one for horticulture, and one for creative arts. The director of Wolfheze notes that once they know their permanent schedules and they can easily carry them out, the residents relax and are free to be themselves. He sees the predictability of the setting as providing a calming influence and reports that previous violent behaviors are significantly reduced in frequency or intensity. At Wolfheze "it's all right to be autistic," while at Kannerhuis, emphasis is on treatment to improve social skills and decrease autistic behaviors. Here, pressure is off the residents to continually learn new behaviors or substitute different behaviors.

Programming for residents at Wolfheze continues into the evening. Monday night there is leisure time to pursue personal hobbies; Tuesday is the night for sporting activities in town, along with the Kannerhuis students. On Wednesday night there is a choice between bake-club, where residents gather in the recreation room to participate in making cookies or cakes and then share the treat, or creativity where a variety of crafts are offered in a well stocked art room. Thursday night they gather for music and dancing. And on Friday everyone views the video Journal that has been taped throughout the week at Wolfheze. They use this opportunity to review the week's activities. Weekends are unscheduled, so staff and residents can decide together between activities like walking, hiking, or shopping.

One of the Wolfheze staff reemphasized the benefits of this setting with an example of the successful transition of a young man who had had difficulties at Kannerhuis. He had been moved in and out of many temporary foster homes throughout his childhood. When he lived at Kannerhuis and saw fellow residents move on to other houses as they progressed, he felt insecure about where he would live and was very anxious about the possibility of being moved again. As a result, he would have violent tantrums and crash his head against the wall. When he was ultimately moved to Wolfheze and understood that it would be his home forever, there was a dramatic change in his behavior. Tantrums stopped completely. He became actively involved in all activities at Wolfheze and remains a generally good humored, talkative, and involved citizen in that community.

Parents of young people with autism seem to have mixed views of Wolfheze.

Father: I think about Wolfheze that nobody has the idea that it is just a part of an open community. I'm not sure of it, but I think there are still big fences around it.
Interviewer: Would you like your child to be there?
Mother: Yes, yes.
Interviewer: What do you think is good about it?
Mother: He is for the rest of his life protected, and they have things to do during the day time and in the evening; and as a parent you need not worry about things.
Interviewer: How do you feel?
Father: That is, of course, your biggest worry, about where he is when we aren't there anymore. Of course, that's a major worry.

A Participant-Observer's Perspective

Tonie Broekhuijsen, a journalist with *Margriet* (1988) magazine, spent a week at Wolfheze to get an inside view of life there. She learns of the resident Hermien's perseverative and anxiety-ridden experiences, as she accompanies her to town to buy a gift and visit the hairdresser. Hermien talks continually, repeating herself over and over:

Hermien: Are we going by train or by car, Tonie?
Tonie: What you like best? I don't care.
Hermien: Let's go by train, Tonie. Or shall we go by car?
Tonie: If you like the train better, we'll go by train.
Hermien: But we can also go by car, Tonie?
Tonie: You tell me.
Hermien: The train or the car?

Such ambiguities make Hermien stiffen with tension. She taps her middle finger against her temple and tightens her jaw. When Tonie decides they will go by car, she finally relaxes. As they walk to the parking lot—"I would have liked the train also, Tonie."

On another occasion Hermien is given the opportunity to be more independent. She makes a date with a group leader to meet in the train station of another city so they can go shopping together. Hermien arrives first. She panics and becomes agitated when she doesn't see the other woman. She becomes upset with everyone around her until the railway police must intervene. She completely forgets that she has two coins and the telephone number in her pocket and has been instructed to call home if difficulties arise.

Hermien's mother tells the journalist of her child's early development and the professional help sought. It wasn't an easy decision to place Hermien in the workhouse. Hermien is twenty years old and has already been in institutions for eighteen of those years.

When she was two years old she searched for "dark places" in her room. As a three year old she screamed day and night, but nobody understood why. Hermien was an attention-getting child in other ways, too. She didn't chew her food, didn't speak, and refused to be held. Finally, the doctor advised her family to put her in an observation clinic, where the diagnosis was made. Hermien's mother said it was not an easy decision to let Hermien go:

> . . . but we didn't have any choice. We couldn't give her what she could get in the psychiatric institutions in Amersford,

and the Dr. Leo Kannerhuis in Oosterbeek namely, attention, much attention.

Hermien came to us on the weekends and during vacation. It wasn't easy. She can be very fatiguing for the family. She needed constant attention. If you took her to a store, you had to know what mood she was in because she was capable of terrible scenes and tantrums. She doesn't understand changes at home.

Now she comes home for a weekend once every three weeks. It's more giving than taking, but in her own way, Hermien can be very cozy. She likes playing games together and she will feel at ease and talk while she is washing the dishes.

I have to be happy about that because no matter how difficult the contact is, she is still my child.

What is Ahead?

Changes are ahead at both the Dr. Leo Kannerhuis and Wolfheze. As the Dr. Leo Kannerhuis looks to the future, it faces new issues in its own developmental progress. A new director must be chosen, someone with business skills who can manage the large budget now assigned to the ever-growing program. Previous leadership was in the hands of people skilled in areas of mental health and program design, but now business acumen is required and more valued.

The new leadership must deal with changing governmental policies in times of financial strain. There will be more competition between institutions as the government tries to increase quality, or at least maintain current levels, while decreasing costs. Until this time, residential youth psychiatry has been one of the best financed services in the field of National Mental Health Care. This is expected to change within the next two years according to van Belle-Bakker (1992).

As better ambulatory treatment care is developed throughout Holland for children and adolescents with autism, the referral of more severely impaired and complicated cases is expected and probably unavoidable. How will programming at Kannerhuis change to accommodate this population? How will they decide who stays at Kannerhuis?

Will they use diagnostic test criteria? Interviews of parents and candidates? Trial periods of residency? Can there be movement back and forth between settings? How will they prepare for after-care needs? How many more long-term care programs are needed in Holland? Will the Wolfheze model be altered in any significant ways? Shortly, some residents from Kannerhuis will spend their days at Wolfheze, learning to participate in the work center there.

Planning continues for far-reaching goals to create a standard curriculum for job-training as well as for social skills, self-help and leisure time skill training. In its well-organized fashion, the staff at Kannerhuis works to anticipate and cope with important changes that are ahead. With Kannerhuis' prominence and success come questions: Can it become too big? Might the administrators find themselves too distant from direct service staff? Are the residents challenged by too much pressure? And at Wolfheze, we might ask: Is maintenance a resident's only hope? Is there any way to minimize the stigma of living in that location? How can more interaction with the outside community be achieved?

Finally, it must be reemphasized that the methodical and careful, organized nature of the Kannerhuis culture fits with the behavioral model. The sense of order which prevails is a solid environment for programmed learning and the constant use of rewards and incentives to shape and encourage behavior change. The flexibility of the Dutch system, by contrast, is nowhere seen more vividly than in the relaxed and comfortable atmosphere of Wolfheze. We await the results of the planned research into the satisfaction of living at the workhome in contrast with life at other psychiatric facilities.

Ny Allerødgård
Allerød, Denmark

Origins

Ny Allerødgård is Scandinavia's only farmstead community for adults with autism. It was created within the rich
and very human influences of Danish history and culture, by
a nation whose fundamental values include democracy, egal-
itarianism, moderation and balance, social welfare and social responsibility (Borish, 1991).

The philosophy of Søren Kierkegaard contributed to that
culture the theory that each human being is unique, has
needs, and should have the ability to satisfy those needs.
(Andersen, 1990, p. 13). The founders of Ny Allerødgård felt
that the frustration of personal needs was dehumanizing to
individuals. Respect for personal needs, values, and goals,
coupled with realistic and humane expectations for development, were essential elements of their philosophy. This
living-working-learning setting is guided by principles of
environmental therapy which require a common goal—
effective communications between all parties involved and
strong ties between staff and parents.

Mogens Andersen (1992), Director of Ny Allerødgård,
vividly recalls the crowded life in a large Danish psychiatric
institution where he was a teacher twenty years ago. There,
among the 1,200 inhabitants with all kinds of mental handicaps, children were herded about in groups of twenty. They
had nothing of their own—no clothing that was theirs, no
possessions. No toys were available for play. No programs
were planned. Recreation consisted of wandering around an
empty yard. They slept in a large dormitory with twenty
beds, watched over by one staff member. When children

turned eighteen, they were sent to locked hospital units where life was even more restricted.

Some of those among the emotionally disturbed patients at such a hospital appeared to Mogens to be different from the others. They were either hyperactive and easily over-stimulated or else quite withdrawn. And with these "different" patients, he founded the first class for children with autism within the state institution. He learned from Else Hansen, a teacher and founder of Denmark's first school for children with autism, how to create a structured environment for them. In spite of a strongly psychoanalytically-oriented state system, Else Hansen had begun to use behavioral teaching methods in the early 1960s. She was the parent of a daughter with autism and had created Sofieskolen as a place where pupils with autism could learn and change. In 1972 she visited Mogens' class each week to supervise and guide him in the use of structured teaching techniques. Her advice to him was to avoid doing exactly what she was doing, rather to understand why she did it and to find his own way.

Although she may have been misunderstood in her own time because of her strong emphasis on structure, Mogens believes that Else Hansen advocated a genuinely human-istic view. She emphasized the importance of knowing and understanding the autistic person with whom you are work-ing, respecting that person's needs, and combining sensitiv-ity and intuition along with good teaching. Insisting on structure in teaching and learning can result in battles with students, Mogens says. He believes that "battles are always a symptom of not finding a good way to do things."

He envisioned a better life for those pupils with autism he had identified, and imagined a farm where they could live and work. Of the 100 identified, he selected ten who would be the first in his new community. Else Hansen and the pu-pils' parents helped the dream of Ny Allerødgård become a reality.

We should not forget, either, the efforts of Psykotiske Børns Vel, Landsforening for Autister, the Danish national autism society. Created in 1962, this association now has 1,232 members including parents, friends of people with au-tism and professionals. Their objectives are to support parents, establish pre-school programs, schools, workshops and living facilities, and to encourage research into autism. They believe strongly that malfunction of the central nervous system underlies autistic disorders and consider psychogenic explanation to be invalid (Autism Europe Association, 1992, p. 14). They also work as a political force at the county and municipal levels to influence legislation and funding for their projects.

The development of Ny Allerødgård also occurred at the time of decentralization of the large institutions in Denmark. By 1980 control of social services for those with mental disorders was handed over from the Danish national government to the counties. Fortunately, the counties were eager to undertake this responsibility.

The first group of parents raised funds to purchase land, and soon discovered that the municipality of Allerød had a historical site which it wished to preserve. This site was located half an hour north of Copenhagen, about one and one-half miles from Allerød's town center. The municipality leased the land and a 100-year-old farm house complex to the parent group, at the same time that the county government was prepared to pay for the operations of the facility.

Two parents remember well those early complicated and exciting efforts:

Interviewer: Tell me about the founding of Ny Allerødgård.

Father: Mogens must tell himself how he got interested in autism. We didn't talk about autism at that time, we called it "psychotic" at that time, yes. But at the time, around 1980, he could see a possibility of creating a place for certain young people who otherwise would end up in closed wards. And he collected, assembled, a group of parents of children that he knew from his pre-school education; I think parents of say, fifteen young people, and asked them if they would go into this job, and they accepted.

Mother: Well-knowing that there would only be room for ten of the young people from the beginning.

Father: So it turned out. But .. the parents agreed and Mogens suggested that we set up three committees: One called the house committee, one called the educational pedagogial committee, and one called the economic committee which also took care of the legal questions. And they each went into how such an institution could be set up within Frederiksborg County which was the political landscape. The housing committee went around all the county to find a suitable building. The pedagogical group went into what should take place in such a program and how you could combine a dwelling and education and work, and the economical committee went into the legal side of the matter. What were the possibilities within legislation, and how could it be paid for and what would the budget be?

Interviewer: Was there a framework within the government that permitted it at the time?

Father: Yes. The law of social assistance permits public support of self-owning institutions. And, we found out that it is possible for a group of parents to set up an institution and arrange for the initial costs to be met. Then the public takes the running costs over.

Interviewer: Parents paid for the land and the property?

Father: Well, they didn't pay for it themselves, but they arranged to raise funds.

Interviewer: So it was private funds that bought the land and property.

Father: Well, we didn't actually buy the land because in our search the housing groups asked the various municipalities within the county what possibilities there would be, and a representative of one of the municipalities said, "As a matter of fact, we have some buildings that we don't know what to do with. They should be saved because they have a certain historic interest to our area. The land has now been taken over by the public to be subdivided into dwellings and agricultural purposes, the buildings are left over and we really don't know what to do with them. At the moment they are occupied by homeless people."

Interviewer: Homeless people; just camping out?

Father: They were in a terrible state.

Interviewer: The buildings . . . ?

Father: The buildings and the people too. But, we went out and had a look at it and we finally found out that the municipality was interested in saving the buildings, so they would put them in good order outside. What you would call roof, walls and so on. We should get the money to have the inside put in a state so that it could be used as a home and an institution. Then the county would take over the running costs. So it ended up as a self-owning institution supported by the county. But the buildings were let by the municipality to the self-owning institution. So the rent is paid by the county to the institution who pays to the municipality.

Interviewer: Did you have to bring it up to code?

Father: Yes, standards ... exactly. So we found funds that would donate money enough. Especially the installations, the bathrooms and so on, had to be brought in order.

Interviewer: Whose requirements did you follow for that?

Father: There are national standards but they are, in practice, looked after by the county doctor.

Interviewer: Inspected by the doctor?

Father: And, of course, the building regulations have to be followed, and they are adopted by the municipality. So there would be various people getting into this.

Interviewer: So the money is coming in to run it. What about the cost per day to run the program?

Father: An annual budget is set up by the County Council on the basis of the number of dwellers, staffing, daily activities, etc. They work to certain standards that apply to other similar places as well. It is the principal's responsibility that expenses do not exceed the budget.

Interviewer: I understand there was much discussion about the staffing.

Father: Yes. Parents have found - and find - staffing scanty.

Interviewer: And about the size?

Father: Well, originally, we were aiming at an institution for ten young people.

Mother: We wouldn't even call it an institution. We called it a home.

Interviewer: And then you expanded the program?

Father: Ny Allerødgård wanted a few rooms fit out as a halfway house; instead, the County Council demanded a regular extension from ten to fifteen dwellers. That has greatly reduced the impression of The Farm as being a home.

Farm House

By 1983, renovations had been made to the sturdy brick building, and Ny Allerødgård welcomed its first ten residents. By 1987, the county added another five residents, and provided financial aid for five day students to attend the program.

As it approaches its tenth anniversary, Ny Allerødgård is the home for fifteen adults with autism who live in three distinct family units within the farm house. Within each family home, five residents have their own bedrooms, and a comfortable, well-lit sitting room to share. Each family group has its own kitchen where breakfast and dinner are prepared and a separate dining area. Five social pedagogues serve as staff for each group of five residents.

The red brick farmhouse is a rather regal building with spacious rooms and large windows that suffuse the interior with bright light. Furnishings are typically Danish. Chairs and tables are spare, light-weight, and attractively designed. Light fixtures are streamlined and multifunctional, and the carpentry, especially in the recently designed kitchen, is hand-finished, attractive, and functional.

The individual rooms are decorated by each student's family, and with the Danish furnishings, each looks more like a sitting room than a counterpart American "bedroom." Beds are fabric-covered foam mattresses on wooden frames with back supports against the wall; they conceal rolled up bedding in order to make the unit appear as a sofa during the day.

A recent addition to the refurbished farm buildings is a large professional-quality stainless steel kitchen designed to meet standards for hotels and restaurants. An adjacent sink and counter area is conveniently located to wash the fruit and vegetables brought in from the farm.

Breakfast and dinner are prepared and eaten in the individual family units, but lunch is made by residents in the large commercial kitchen and served at once to the entire group in the adjacent "canteen." The canteen with its tables and chairs is one of several large spaces available for multiple uses. Morning meetings, for example, are held here, in preparation for the start of each work day.

Other additional large rooms for group gatherings and activities are scattered throughout the building, including a first-floor activity room where folk dancing can take place, and where videos can be projected onto a large screen for weekly group viewing. In the basement, there is an exercise room with a sauna, two classrooms, and a room where eggs and vegetables are sold.

Parents

Parents have always played an important role at Ny Allerødgård. Recall that Mogens Andersen initially had the parents form three committees: the house committee, the pedagogical committee, and the economic and legal committee. They worked within Denmark's law of social assistance which permitted public support of self-owning institutions. Their goals in 1978 were to find a house, develop a budget to run the program, and to decide on policies for helping young adults with autism.

At first they raised the funds to completely renovate the old farm buildings in Allerød. The pedagogical committee explored ways of combining a dwelling, education, and work. The economic committee found possibilities within legislation that would support such a program, and determined what the budget would be. Within only four years' time, they had the project underway.

Since the first ten residents began at Ny Allerødgård in 1982, parents have not abandoned their original critical role. They have formed a parent study group that meets several times a year for mutual support and to learn from invited speakers about different aspects of autism. They contribute to a special fund from which expensive items are bought for the community, such as a large screen T.V. and professional quality VCR that are used for program documentation and pedagogical studies as well as for movies shown every Wednesday night.

Parents continue to visit their adult children and to take them home on appointed weekends, Christmas, Easter, and summer vacations. One possible pattern is to visit at Ny Allerødgård one weekend afternoon and then to take the resident home for the day on the following weekend.

It is no accident that parents think of the "contact person" at Ny Allerødgård as ambassador for their youngster. Each resident is assigned a social pedagogue responsible for oversight of their entire program. His or her role is to support the resident in practical, physical, mental, and developmental matters. This careworker must get along well with both the resident and the resident's family, for communication among these people and the staff is his or her most important function. The contact person learns all about the personality, interests, physical and mental condition, and rituals of the resident so he or she can work out instructions for life-skills training. Responsibility rests with the contact person for passing on this information to new staff and to share as much as possible with parents, who, quite naturally, like to know what's going on in the life of their son or daughter.

The parent contact acts as ambassador in other ways, too. A notebook containing an on-going account of recent significant events is transferred from the contact person to the family in conjunction with visits, and is similarly returned, so there can be some continuity in themes and conversations from the community to home and back again. At regular yearly case conferences, the contact person represents the resident. But some parents revealed that they prefer to hold more frequent meetings. As one explained, "At those treatment meetings once a year, where the doctor is there, the social worker, one person from the county, all those people that you don't know are there. That means that you don't speak about pants or sewing names, or pocket money or flowers or travels . . . Many important things you forget. See, from a parent's point of view, you should maybe begin from the inside out, instead of from the outside in. So that is why we find those four-month meetings much more interesting and close."

Topics covered during those more frequent meetings usually include practical, educational, and family issues of greatest concern to the parents:

I. The general situation
II. Personal development
    -What has changed/is changing since last meeting four months ago?
    -How does staff feel about recent personal development?
    -What new learning can now be encouraged at home?
III. Schooling
IV. Use of spare time
V. Holiday plans
VI. Clothing needs
VII. Pocket money
VIII. Communication between staff and school; staff and parents
IX. Plans for next meeting

Staff

The staff are highly valued at Ny Allerødgård because the care and well-being of each resident, obviously, are the primary concerns. Ny Allerødgård functions under the leadership of the founding Director, Mogens Andersen. He is in charge of program administration, supervises all staff, and maintains relations with parents. As his political and public relations roles have expanded, he has appointed one of the social pedagogues as Assistant Director with responsibilities to take charge when he is out of town. Most of the time and energy of the community's staff is spent in direct contact and service with residents.

Ny Allerødgård prides itself on having carefully trained and experienced personnel in most of these roles. The primary staff consists of five social pedagogues for each family unit of five autistic adults. This staff rotates on shifts throughout days, evenings and weekends, maintaining a ratio of two staff to five residents.

Social pedagogues are trained in Denmark to work in a variety of social welfare services. Their three-year undergraduate course of study in one of the fifteen state colleges of socio-educational training is prerequisite to employment in institutions serving a broad range of physically, mentally, or socially disabled children, adolescents and adults (The Advanced Training Institute, p. 1).

Their curriculum is theoretical as well as practical and prepares them for both psychological and behavioral aspects of their work. Academic subjects students study include Psychology, Pedagogics, Socio-Pedagogics, Social, Health, and Cultural courses as well as activity courses featuring music, drama, sports, and workshops. In the second year an age-specific target group is selected by each student for more intensive focus, while in the third year, a particular area of disability is chosen. Since autism is not offered as a separate topic, those interested would most likely study issues relevant to mental retardation, abnormal psychology, or psychopathology.

Related teaching practice is required for four months of the first year and three months during each of the following two years of study. According to the Skovtofte Socialpædagogiske Seminarium brochure:

> The trainee is to acquire sympathetic and theoretical insight and practical skills in socio-educational work, and a solid foundation for participation in innovatory work within the socio-educational profession.

Additionally,

> The trainee's personal development is to be promoted through occupation with the content of the education.

After several years of work experience, these specialists can qualify for a ten-month leadership training program at the Advanced Training Institute for Social Pedagogues.

In addition to the social pedagogues, Ny Allerødgård employs a joiner to manage the wood crafts program, a farmer who supervises animal care and gardening activities, and a teacher of domestic sciences who supervises food preparation for the noon day meal. A housekeeper cleans the building, although residents are expected to assist in keeping their own rooms neat and orderly. A half-time maintenance individual insures that the facility is in good repair. A half-time bookkeeper and half-time clerk maintain the office, while the equivalent of eight full-time nonprofessional helpers complete the Ny Allerødgård staff.

Two school teachers supplied by the local school district conduct classes within the Ny Allerødgård setting three days each week. In Denmark everyone is guaranteed ten years of schooling, and special education services can extend to adulthood. All the residents at Ny Allerødgård are eligible for this continuing service largely because they have missed several or more years of formal education or have been unable to profit from it in the usual ways because of their learning difficulties. Each resident attends school one day each week so the two teachers work with five or six students at a time.

Since the teachers are not on site all of the time, and with such infrequent attendance, integration of the education program into the larger community is a continuing challenge. The director envisions a time when "lessons for school are lessons for life."

Program

The guiding operational principle of Ny Allerødgård is that school, home, and work are all integrated in one setting. Vocational activities center on wood-craft, farming, and maintaining the home and surrounding property. Tasks selected provide meaningful work for the residents. The pace of activities seems relaxed and unpressured. Staff are gentle and patient with the residents, guiding them through tasks when necessary, but allowing them independence when they are able to perform on their own.

The day begins with breakfast within the individual family units. Then at 8:30 a.m. all residents, day students, and staff assemble for morning meeting in the canteen. Here singing often starts the day and the master schedule, which is displayed on the wall is reviewed so that everyone knows where to go to begin that day's work. Students generally spend the whole day at one activity with varied assignments throughout the week.

The carpentry program is notable, overseen and organized by a professional carpenter. The large well-lit shop is equipped with modern tools adapted with protective devices to assure safety of the workers. A variety of templates and cuing markers have been devised to guide measuring and assembly procedures for the students, and to allow them to assume increasingly greater independence in their woodworking projects.

A wall board displays the variety of wood projects in process in the shop. Items for sale to the public or to specialty stores in the area include a table-top reading or music stand, a four-sided tray, memo boards, and flower boxes.

The carpentry shop is remarkable, too, because drawing from the array of products already begun, the carpenter is able to bring forth the specific project that fits the abilities and interests of the students assigned that day—each finds a niche, so to speak. One young man is able to perform all stages in constructing the music stand now that he has mastered planing, cutting, assembling, and gluing. He attains a satin-smooth finish on the wood, as he routinely counts out fifty strokes while sanding each piece with a uniquely constructed sanding block with a handle.

Reciprocal activity proceeds rhythmically as we see two residents wearing protective goggles plane long rods of wood. The first young man chooses a rod from a pile and starts it through the large electric planer that stands in the middle of the room. The second young man then receives the rod as it exits the machine and stacks it on a shelf nearby. They continue in tandem until they are told to stop for a coffee break.

In the kitchen, attention is given to skill training that will enhance cognitive, social, and personal functions. As the cook supervises four students, they prepare lunch for all, to be served in the canteen. Even without specifically declared objectives or steps in the skills to be taught, she guides each student and fosters increased independence in needed food-preparation tasks. One young woman independently rolls the dough and wraps pieces of it around hot dogs. Another watches the oven as the wrapped hot dogs bake and listens for the timer to ring so she can remove the trays. The students learn through informal behavior modification techniques, from hands-on demonstrations and by gradual fading of assistance in each job. The external reward for these "apprentice" workers is the finished product, ready to be admired, served, and eaten. The obvious outcome of their efforts is providing food for all assembled.

The farmer begins the day attending to the animals. Students working along with him are encouraged to feed the pigs, cows, ducks, and chickens, change their water and clean out the pens. Then all three might drive off together in the truck to purchase feed nearby. As Spring arrives they begin to work in the vegetable garden or greenhouse.

The maintenance staff member works with one resident who assists him in cleaning the freezer. The student's interest in dumping, pouring, and wiping can be easily integrated into this task.

School is held on Monday, Wednesday, and Friday with five or six students in attendance each day. Class begins with a review of those present, calendar activities, and description of the weather. At times the two teachers divide the class to offer some special activities. One leads an exercise program in a room equipped with mats on the floor for two or three of the girls. In a half-hour session, exercises include reciprocal movements, coordination, and relaxation. On other days yoga and eurythmics are introduced.

Academic pursuits include map-making, simple math, and story telling with focus on conversation, especially during coffee breaks. Students learn to make their own coffee and to serve each other appropriately. Since each resident only attends school one day each week, the continuity of curricular topics is difficult to maintain.

When everyone gathers in the canteen for the noon meal, they sit at tables for six and enjoy traditional Danish fare. Lunch might include platters of smørrebrød selections like herring, potato salad, green onions, and paté with a rich variety of hearty breads. Coffee, a popular beverage, is served again at lunch as it was during morning break, and will be again during afternoon break. Those on the kitchen team set the food on the tables and clean up the dishes when the meal is over.

Physical activity out-of-doors is an organic part of the working day, not simply a feature of a leisure and working program. Bikes are available for all, and one of the teachers accompanies one student on a planned long-distance bike ride each week. Several residents and staff jog four to six miles three times a week. The local swimming pool is reserved for the entire group each Friday evening but is also used on Tuesday nights by smaller groups of residents and staff who join with local townspeople for swimming. Four to six residents are taken to nearby stables each week where they both ride and groom the horses. Hikes and long walks are popular pastimes and some often walk the one and a half miles to the center of Allerød and back as they venture forth to buy food and supplies.

Residents and staff alike look forward to their regularly scheduled evening activities. Each Thursday evening the large dining room is cleared for music and folk dancing. Outside guests are often invited to join them. Wednesday evening is movie night. The dining room is set up with rows of chairs, and the new VCR and large screen, purchased by the parents, is used to show a popular video. After the movie, all share a snack that was prepared during the baking session on Monday evening.

The residents of Ny Allerødgård are well known in the community. They often spend time in the town of Allerød for visits to the library or restaurants, for haircuts, or for doctor and dentist appointments. Their yellow van is a familiar sight when they ride into town or off to the country for hikes and picnics. The local community has been educated about the Ny Allerødgård program through the local press and briefings at the library (Andersen, p. 17).

An example of their acceptance is:

> the very good story about some of the young people visiting the shops. Some other customers asked if they would have to

wait until these young people had finished their buying. The owner said, 'If you cannot accept our other customers, you can leave.'

To encourage visitors to Ny Allerødgård, an annual open house is held for the townspeople. Many of them return on other occasions to purchase eggs and vegetables from the farm.

Teaching Techniques

Mogens Andersen and the staff at Ny Allerødgård believe in providing a structured environment for adults with autism, but within that structure they treat the residents with a humanistic spirit. Behavior modification is considered a good observation method and a way to eliminate inappropriate behavior, but teaching of new skills is often accomplished through an intuitive sense of the preferences and abilities of the residents—getting "inside their skin," one might say. General aims are to teach involvement, social responsibility, and independent thinking while nurturing self-esteem, love, friendship, and basic trust.

It is not easy to categorize the philosophy of treatment in this Danish program. In reality it is flexible, eclectic, and relies on personal judgment and intuition. There is respect for individuality in guidance, decision making, and teaching. The cooperative, sensitive, and caring staff attitude minimizes confrontation or direct conflict, and highlights doing what works for the residents. Their kind and gentle insistence, for example, was effective for Kirk who was not interested in jogging. He was at first carried from the starting line to the end of the track. Gradually, he began to participate and now jogs enthusiastically several times each week.

While the environment is well structured and generally predictable, the staff are able to introduce a variety of new activities and experiences on and off the premises. They have even traveled abroad with residents several times as far as Norway for skiing and Greece for a holiday!

In recent years the staff at Ny Allerødgård have been impressed with the program of sequential visualization described to them in 1990 by Dr. Gary Mesibov of the University of North Carolina, USA, TEACCH Program (see also Schopler & Mesibov, 1983 and 1985). They have tried this technique with one of their most difficult students and have had positive results. Now they are expanding this picture-cuing system to others at Ny Allerødgård (see Giddan and Giddan, 1984 and 1991). The technique involves extensive visual cuing for each step in each task. The student gradu-ally learns to carry out the task independently by looking at and following the sequence in the series of pictures.

They describe the transformation of Eric through this approach. Eric was very difficult to manage and would often wander away. He would become very violent and they had a hard time keeping him on the premises. He was very com-pulsively interested in small ceramic beads and would often run away and go to a local kindergarten, take their beads, and bring them back to his room. They had a lot of difficulty with him. Several years ago they heard Dr. Mesibov speak at a conference in Denmark, where he told about the visualiza-tion approach in use at TEACCH. Mogens said that it was the most impressive thing he had heard in his twenty years in this work. The staff implemented the visualization tech-nique with Eric. They began by teaching him his routine of the day and his daily schedule. Then they taught him the cooking routines through the use of pictures, placed on vel-cro pages, that he could remove when he finished each task. A video tape of Eric shows that, when accompanied, he is able to go to the super market, use his reference book of pic-tures, and select the right food in the right amount. After he has put each food item in his shopping cart, he takes the pic-ture of it, and sticks it on the back of the book. He also has to weigh the produce and put the tag on it, bring all the food up to the check-out counter, unload it onto the counter, pay for the food, pack it into the bag, and then put the bag into his back-pack for the return to Ny Allerødgård. He then fol-lows a picture recipe in the kitchen and is able to indepen-dently go through the many, many steps of making his weekly ratatouille. In the video tape he is excited, animated, and keeps saying to himself, "very good, very good." It seems to be a powerful, self-motivating, well-structured, and self-rewarding experience for him, and he seems to feel quite pleased.

Picture cues at Ny Allerødgård now appear at each bedroom doorway where the activities of that individual's day are displayed in chronological order. Photos appear in the bathroom to guide toileting and bathing procedures. They appear in the kitchen to allow residents to determine what food supplies need to be replaced, and food pictures are placed on velcro-studded pages as a shopping list for all those who can go to the grocery store. Pictures guide cooking procedures for baking and for dinner recipes that can be produced without direct supervision.

Incorporating this technique has required the staff to think more critically about the specific order of steps to be learned and performed in each task. It has focused them on rewarding mastery of small increments of behavior and has enhanced their commitment to what they call "sequential support" techniques for new learning. The staff has even discovered that some residents who previously had frequent violent temper outbursts now seem more focused and under better control. When they can be successful in complicated tasks that interest them, they appear more content.

The administration learned through some difficulties in the early years that it is better not to group together those residents who need the most attention. More success was achieved when they divided those most difficult to manage among the three family living units. Both staff and fellow residents seemed to benefit from the change. But temper outbursts and potential violence remain an issue for staff intervention at Ny Allerødgård just as they are at most other settings for adults with autism (see Berney, 1992).

The philosophy here is to confront the problem before it escalates and to remove the distressed resident from the others as quickly as possible. From fellow workers who have had more experience, staff members learn techniques for interrupting different kinds of inappropriate or dangerous behaviors. They believe it is often effective to immediately use language to process what has taken place as a way to clarify and rectify any misunderstanding.

Staff: As you saw this morning Poul threw a tantrum when we were at the morning meeting. He threw the tantrum because Jens, whom you've met, usually comes up and helps me in the unit for an hour, from 8:00 to 9:00, and he couldn't do it this morning because he had to be somewhere else, and somebody else was throwing a tantrum at that time. Poul when he throws a tantrum, is very often self-destructive, but today he chose to hold one of the other people by the arm. He has got rather sharp nails so he can scratch a bit. She screamed. In the six months I've been here, what I've worked personally with is not letting other people's fear affect me. What I do when Poul erupts in that way, I try to look him in the eye and try to hold him lightly on the hand. We've talked a lot about this in our group, sometimes we've tried other things. Basically, we feel physical contact should be tried—nothing like pulling and shoving—and then we have some catch phrases we use.

Interviewer: Different ones for different people?

Staff: No, we try to use the same ones. We ask him what the problem is: "What is your problem?" And very often that works. And then he usually says something that doesn't really grasp meaning, or sentences, or very often hits himself on the head or does something else, but if you ask again, you would eventually come to some sort of practical problem that he has got. Today he said Jens wasn't up in the unit at 8:00, and luckily I knew why Jens wasn't there. I was able to give him a precise account of where Jens was, after which I got Poul to sit down again and look at the board which says where everyone is and what everyone is doing for the rest of the day. I got him to tell me where he was on the board and what he was going to do.

While unpredictable and difficult to manage behaviors require continued vigilance and prompt intervention in residential settings such as this, sexual behaviors are also an important concern. In their national study of adults with autism in group homes in Denmark, Haracopos and Pedersen (1992) suggest that behavioral problems can occur in connection with unresolved sexual difficulties. Their findings were gathered through questionnaires filled out by staff members responsible for each resident, with consultation from other staff. Eighty-one Danish adults with autism

were surveyed—fifty-seven men and twenty-four women—
with an average age of 25.8 years.

The complex findings confirmed or provided some support for the survey's five principal hypotheses:

1. Sexual behavior is a common occurrence among people with autism.
2. Sexual behavior is often expressed in an inappropriate way for the surroundings and for the people with
   autism themselves.
3. Sexual behavior is expressed in a deviant and bizarre
   way in relation to the accepted norm.
4. Behavioral problems occur in connection with unresolved sexual problems.
5. People with autism are unable to establish or have
   difficulty in establishing a sexual relationship.

The Danes confront these issues directly, at the residential level through staff inservice training, and nationally,
through governmental brochures concerning the management of violent behavior and sexual issues in special
populations.

A Glance Ahead

As Ny Allerødgård celebrates its tenth anniversary it
aims toward growth of the farm complex to include the addition of a store where produce and crafts can be sold. Future plans are being considered for establishment of a group
home, with ties to Ny Allerødgård, for residents who seem
able to live more independently. And efforts will be made to
create an information center on autism.

Old and new questions will need to be answered. Can
those who develop and learn successfully at Ny Allerødgård
move on to a more independent living arrangement? Will
there be enough well-supervised group homes or apartments
available for those who need them? How shall Ny Allerødgård grow in the future? Might other farm communities
be created in Scandinavia to extend this program to more

adults with autism, developmental disabilities, or mental retardation? Can the parents "let go" and sufficiently trust that their children will be adequately protected, nurtured, and challenged in the years ahead? Will the founding Director be able to juggle all his roles as administrator, political lobbyist, and spokesperson for autism? Will other leaders need to be groomed to take up the slack? Will there be continuity of care for the future? If the past tells us anything about the future, all of these questions will be faced straightforwardly and answered honestly by all of the Ny Allerødgård constituencies—residents, parents, families, staff, government, and local community.

There are concerns, too, that as economic constraints continue, the government might shift its focus and provide less support. For these reasons, the Director and his professional colleagues continue to educate politicians about the merits of such settings. They favor reduction in the governmental bureaucracy overseeing these programs as a substitute for any direct financial cut-backs in their operations.

Considerable sums are involved in this debate over funding. The daily cost of supporting each adult at Ny Allerødgård ranges from $240 for residents to $160 for day students. Of the total annual budget, personnel costs ($1,087,200) are three times the outlay for operating expenses ($317,100). Currently, the project continues to be completely supported by government funds at a level comparable to other similar settings.

In summary, the Danes' ten year record of strong commitment is quite admirable. Their careful analysis of future directions reflects an attitude of empathy and caring about residents and families, but also reflects their hands-on social and political knowledge and influence. Future leadership needs cultivation and training, so that parents and families may be assured that this high quality program will continue. Non-aversive behavioral teaching methods such as sequential support have great promise here and could be applied more frequently and more widely.

Britain - Somerset Court;
Ireland - Dunfirth Community;
Germany - Hof Meyerwiede;
and Spain - La Garriga

Where did the farmstead models of Britain, Ireland, Germany, and Spain begin? What were some early educational and medical influences upon this form of care, demonstrated by Somerset Court, Dunfirth, Hof Meyerwiede, and La Garriga, for those with physical and mental disability?

We look to the legacy of Rudolf Steiner (1955), the Austrian philosopher, who in 1924 began to describe his Curative Educational approach. He had arrived at this method through his own early experiences. As a young student in 1886, Steiner had been employed as a tutor for a family with four sons. The youngest son was ten years old, "abnormal in his physical and mental development with alarming emotional behavior" (Steiner, 1977). He might have been a child with autism.

Steiner created a highly structured teaching program and provided the child with daily lessons. After bringing him up to grade level, he encouraged the family to allow the youth to attend school with other children. His individual tutoring continued after school. Steiner's feeling that the boy had intellectual potential was verified as his young charge succeeded in school, eventually went on to complete his education in medicine, and became a physician.

Perhaps from this experience, Steiner (1955, p. 9) evolved his Curative Education approach. He believed in an "attitude of reverence for the human individuality in itself, irrespective of its outer achievements in life." He referred to the handicapped child as "the child in need of special soul-care" and in his lectures on the subject in 1924, said that such a child "can unfold to its fullest extent, and frustration can give way to a feeling of its own value and worth in life as it meets with an understanding directed not only towards its handicaps, but towards its true self."

Steiner (1955) had a profound influence on homes created for children with all degrees of physical and mental disabilities, and schools for those who were expected to return to the normal school life after a period of treatment. The approaches used in those homes and schools included the following elements (p. 10):

1. A rhythmical way of living in beautiful and harmonious surroundings as a background for medical and educational treatment.
2. Lessons incorporating living and imaginative presentation of subject matter adapted to individual requirements and capacities in which music, painting, handwork, and so on would help the children unfold their natural talents.
3. Medical treatment with remedial exercises, medicinal baths, special medicaments, diet, and massage, all of which would "enliven and strengthen the growing organism."

The model spread to Britain where in the early 1930s several children's homes were built. In 1939 the first of the Camphill-Rudolf Steiner Schools was created for children in need of special care. It was staffed by a groups of doctors, teachers, nurses, and artists under the direction of Dr. Karl König. By 1955 the Camphill Program had grown to include 250 boys and girls, serving "children and young people unable to follow curriculum of ordinary schools because of mental or physical disability." The program also cared for children and adolescents with emotional problems. Today the scope of the Camphill movement is international. In Britain it extends to schools for children age six to fourteen, further education colleges for those fifteen to early twenties, and adult villages. In each Camphill center people with many different forms of mental handicaps live in communities with permanent co-workers who carry out the tasks of teaching and working, in the house and on the land. All are called upon to find their place in the community, and each person is appreciated as having special needs and gifts. Work is focused on the land, housework, and a wide variety of crafts (National Autistic Society, 1991).

According to Karst (1991), the work of Bockoven (1963) and Elgar (1991) also point us to the contemporary developments of farmstead communities, the most widely known and imitated of which is Somerset Court. In addition to Somerset Court, other British non-urban residential settings for those with autism include Middle Field Manor, Dereham Autistic Community, High Croft, Longford Court, Peldon Old Rectory, Raby Hall Community, St. Erme House and Whitegates (National Autistic Society, 1988). By comparison, autism is just now being identified in children in Korea, the former Yugoslavia, and Czechoslovakia, and the needs of adults with autism are receiving increased attention in Israel and Italy.

The following brief tour of four communities will touch on both their similarities and differences. These centers for adults with autism are: Somerset Court in Somerset, England, Dunfirth Community in Enfield, County Kildare, Ireland, Hof Meyerwiede in Grinden, near Bremen, Germany, and La Garriga, outside Barcelona, Spain. Similarities involve deinstitutionalization, parental influence and organization, local and national government financing and provision of resources, a preference for rural farmstead settings, and some likenesses in age and range of abilities of residents with autism. The differences are seen in size, programming, staff training, record keeping, degree of individualized education and treatment, and expectations of staff and parents for more-or-less permanent living arrangements. It might be useful to occassionally refer to the key variables shown in Appendix D in order to clarify the material presented in the following comparisons.

Purpose and Background

These programs were founded because there was a lack of appropriate services for adults with autism in each country. Alternatives had included locked wards in state-run institutions or inadequate care and attention for adults with autism when placed among large groups of patients with mental retardation and other severe disturbances. In these countries, the types of services represented by the farmstead projects were unprecedented.

Each of the programs has relatively similar goals. The concerns of each center are for the care and treatment of adults with autism and expanding their access to as wide a range of life experiences as possible.

Britain's Somerset Court stresses "a secure, stable environment through which interventions directed towards the Triad of Impairments can be programmed." Ireland's Dunfirth Community focuses on "a recognition of the individuality of persons with autism, their capacity to benefit from education, training, and care, and their entitlement to participate in the development of the society in accordance with their individual capacity and dignity as human beings." A concise and specific operational characterization of their country's only farmstead community has been given to us by the Irish Society for Autism (1989):

> Dunfirth Autistic Community is an alternative to life-long institutionalization in psychiatric hospitals. The setting is a farm on seventy acres, three miles from the nearest village. At Dunfirth, the residents live in houses grouped around a courtyard, in an atmosphere which combines care with maximum freedom. They live and work as a traditional farm family would—tending livestock, growing vegetables, rearing poultry, cutting timber and saving turf. They contribute in a large way to the success and self-sufficiency of the community and are fulfilled themselves. Sawing timber and carrying fodder are healthier ways of using energy than pacing from wall to wall in a hospital recreation room.
>
> Dunfirth sells produce to the people of the locality, from poultry to vegetables, to concrete pavers and garden furniture.

From Germany we learn that:

> Hof Meyerwiede is an alternative to the traditional placement for handicapped adults in Germany (living in a residen-

tial home—working in large sheltered workshops—doing always identical small tasks). The farm-life provides a structure determined by the rhythm of nature, the needs of animals and plants and the residents themselves. The farm represents a therapeutic environment with meaningful work. All the work has to be done and so it is done by the residents together with the staff. Another important goal of the setting is the involvement of the parents.

La Garriga, in Spain, working with a younger population, aims towards "the best possible attention for the autistic person so that they can continue to form part of their family." A plan for the treatment and education of adults with autism in Spain has been developed by Rom and Cuxart (1987) under the sponsorship of the Fundació Tutelar Congost Autisme, which stresses this basic principle:

> The maintenance of the severely affected autistic adult under dignified conditions in his or her own family and social environment in accordance with the basic principles of human constitutional and even legal rights (p. 17).

The plan distinguishes between adults with autism who have received treatment since infancy and those who have not. For those who have received treatment, the plan envisages the need for work and a regular occupation, if possible, for continued support, and for adequate institutions so that "psychiatric internment" is avoided. To the extent possible, continued life within the adult's nuclear family is envisioned, as long as it is beneficial to the individual with autism.

These issues of job, support, and family life are seen as typically more complex for those who have not received treatment in childhood. For them, it would be more difficult to avoid so-called "psychiatric internment" and the institutions designed to help them would reflect a more complex organization. In sum, the plan's emphasis for this group is on 1) work in adequate circumstances, 2) continued therapy and support by expert staff to avoid regression, 3) adequate institutions to avoid "psychiatric internment", and 4) living in one's nuclear family. Practical and realistic, the plan anticipates orienting politicians and administrators toward environments for adults with autism which are therapeutic and supportive, which have appropriate technical staff, and in which there is continuity between different components.

The British, Irish, German, and Spanish programs were all founded by parent (and therapist) groups and national societies inspired by strong leadership and sustained by a collective will to initiate and change services and programs. While the parent leadership and impetus may be seen as an indirect critique of professionals and governments, at the same time the process has resulted in a blend of private sponsorship, government support, and parental leadership as the general rule. Can such a social and political movement, or trend, continue itself? Can we count on new generations of parents to sustain or re-establish such a commitment?

It is impossible to consider these programs without acknowledging and giving credit to the respective national and regional autism societies that either created or are responsible for these settings now. In Britain, the National Autistic Society (NAS) was created in 1962 and has about 2,500 members, two thirds of whom are parents and the rest professionals and friends. There are about fifty local societies, independent but affiliated, which have a further 8,000 members with the same ratio of parents, professionals, and friends. The National Society is currently being restructured with a view to assigning various responsibilities to seven newly created regions. The NAS runs seven residential schools and six residential communities. The affiliated societies operate another nine schools and twenty-one residential communities, many of which also provide day care facilities. A team of thirty salaried workers is employed at the head office. Projects at hand include a center for diagnosis and an expansion of political activity in the care field. Their publications include numerous pamphlets and brochures dealing mainly with practical problems, and their journal "Communication" is issued three times a year. "Titles in Autism," a database of research publications and projects, which is also available on diskette, is published for NAS by the University of Sunderland, and is distributed bimonthly.

In Ireland, the Irish Society for Autism (ISA) was created in 1963, and it has available at its head office an information and advisory service, a library, a welcoming service for parents and professionals, and a fund-raising unit. The Society runs a residential home for twenty young adults, a weekday boarding school for ten to twelve children (not yet operational due to financial difficulties) while a home providing complete service for twenty adults was opened in 1991. The Society also plays a part in the management of a home for five adolescents, in two others for five and four adults respectively, in a work center for twenty-two adults and in a training center for ten young adults. The problem of special education which the ISA cannot assist is one which needs urgent attention in Ireland.

The founder-association of Germany's Hof Meyerwiede is "Hilfe für das autistische Kind Bremen—Help for the Autistic Child—(HAK, Bremen), a non-profit organization that includes only parents and therapists. The regional association is part of the national association of the *Bundersverband* "Hilfe für das autistische Kind" (HAK). Begun by parents in 1970 as a West German Association, HAK Bundersverband now includes twenty-five regional societies, with a total membership of 2,500. Its main objectives have been to create a unified approach to specialized treatment of children with autism and to support and advise parents. Home-based treatment was preferred by this group, so while twenty institutions were created to serve these children, the majority would live with their families. To disseminate information, HAK has published texts about autism, distributed pamphlets, especially to physicians, and organized conferences, training courses, and seminars for teachers. It also provides advice to parents by telephone. In the last few years it has begun to create homes for adolescents and adults with autism.

HAK, Bremen has created the Bremen project which has grown since 1972 to include a special class for autistic children (1976), and an ambulatory center opened in 1977 that now includes a staff of seven with psychologists, sociologists and ergotherapists. They serve thirty children and provide early diagnosis, early intervention, ambulant therapy, continuous instruction, and family therapy. Hof Meyerwiede was opened in 1988 to provide community life for adults with autism.

In Germany, diagnosis of autism can be made by some child psychiatrists at university clinics, although they are not specialists in that field. Education for those children diagnosed might take place in the few specially designated classes attached to schools for children with mental handicaps or for those with emotional disturbances. "The school situation is reported to be unsatisfactory" (Demeestere & Van Buggenhout, p. 173).

Care services are limited to five special residential homes and three small communities where adults with autism can live and work. For children there are nineteen ambulant teams managed by regional autism societies offering home-based therapy, and one day-care center for children with autism in Hannover.

There are no workshop settings for adults with autism, and because of the difficult economic situation in Germany, no improvement is expected in either educational or vocational opportunities for this population (Demeestere & Van Buggenhout, p. 176).

Several Spanish societies and groups have begun notable activities (Autism-Europe Association, 1992). Associació de Pares Amb Fills Autistes i Caracterials de Catalunya (APAFACC) was founded in 1976 and is made up of parents and professional members. It set up different departments and entities which now form a network whose objective is to meet all the needs of those with autism throughout their lives. At La Garriga, APAFACC has created the CERAC center for children of school age, the TERLAB center for adults, and the residence LLAR CAU BLANC.

In the rest of Catalonia, L'associació de Pares Amb Fills Autistes de Mataro i Comarca and L'associació de Pares Amb Nens Psicòtics Autistes de L'Anoia hope to improve the training and quality of life of individuals with autism by maximizing the application of technical progress in the interests of these people. The Spanish Association of Autistic Children's Parents (APNA), founded in 1976, today includes 400 parents from all over the Spanish territory. The association is made up of parents, professionals, and friends, but all the members of the Council are parents of children with autism. The centers they have created include Leo Kanner, a day education center for twenty-four pupils, and Belvis, an education center for sixteen pupils from various Spanish provinces. Residences they have built are Belvis, a permanent residence during the school year for students from the Belvis center, and M. Isabel Bayonas, a permanent residence for adults with autism due to start its activities in 1992. It has a capacity for thirty residents, and fifteen adults during the day. Construction of a farm-workshop in Villatobas has just begun.

Direct services that are available from APNA include diagnosis and orientation, early attention, ambulatory therapy, summer hostels, training courses for parents, intensive 5-day seminars for qualified staff, yearly 9-month theoretical and practical courses for university professionals to get specialized in autism, and conferences. The headquarters offers a secretary and general manager, a library, a video rental shop, social and cultural activities, fund raising activities, an investigation office, an information center, a department of partners, collaborators and members, as well as an accountant's and treasurer's office.

The Association works with the Civil Service regarding advice and training of its technical staff in the field of autism. APNA has promoted the foundation and the setting up of other associations within the national borders as well as in Latin America by providing them with its support, experience and advice.

GAUTENA is the Autistic Society of Guipuzcoa representing the Basque Country in northern Spain. Founded in 1978, it currently has 150 members, all of whom are parents or other relatives of the clients. The aims of the Association are to provide or otherwise procure diagnosis, attention, education, accommodation, and training for people with autism and other pervasive developmental disorders, in the least restrictive environment. It is subsidized almost entirely by the local authorities.

GAUTENA is responsible for the running of one school, as well as nine special classes which are integrated in regular schools. It sponsors a Day Activity Center for adults, a sheltered flat offering full time accommodation, and a hostel which offers weekend respite care. Psychiatric services are also provided, including diagnosis, follow-up, and outpatient treatment, which is subsidized by the Basque Health Service. Respite care, family support, and leisure activities are other important aspects of their work. Altogether, about 100 clients are served, although not all of them have autism.

Future plans include a group home (opening 1992) for twelve youngsters. They also aim to develop schemes by which to supervise the process of integration of students with autism into regular schools, resolve the question of legal protection for clients, and promote social awareness.

Funding and Leadership

The financing of these programs is an interesting mix of public and private funds. The English program for 43 residents is completely financed with public funds. Budgets are estimated according to the need for individual services. In 1992 the cost for each resident was £628 ($1,237) per week. Operating expenses including wages and benefits were £995,136 ($1,960,000) while operating expenses totaled £436,463 ($860,000). This level of support was considered adequate for the year's operation. For voluntary or independent services, these budgets range in the upper middle cost bracket, but when compared with private and statutory agencies, they seem low.

The Dunfirth project for twenty-two residents, like most centers for those with mental handicaps in Ireland, is only partly supported with public funds. Each year the Irish Society for Autism must raise substantial sums to supplement the budget. This year the public contribution was £420,000 ($788,000) and private donations reached £50,000 ($93,800). This was not considered adequate support as money was not available to provide the needed professional expertise. At Dunfirth £380,000 ($712,880) was paid for wages and benefits while £90,000 ($168,840) covered operating expenses.

Hof Meyerwiede, which has eleven residents (8 male and 3 female) and a total budget of more than half a million dollars, is funded completely by public funds through the Social Ministry of Bremen and Niedersachsen. Private funding through HAK Bremen helps pay for furniture, buildings, and equipment. Specifically, the budget for personnel is $438,480 and operating expenses, $146,160. The per diem cost for each resident is $168.08. Generally, it is felt that there is adequate budgetary support and salaries, and Herr Cordes reports:

> But it is probable that our farm is more expensive than other settings. We need more staff (our overall ratio is 2:1), but we have a very small budget for administration. (Most work is done by non-profit-salary work of the board of HAK!).

It is estimated to cost about $40,000 a year to support each of the forty individuals within the program at La Garriga. The Spanish community is funded by private individual contributions and other private and public sources.

Several settings have differentiated staff and leadership roles while others employ staff as needed. At Somerset Court the Principal is responsible for operational management of the facility including development of programs and service quality. There are four assistant managers, two for day programs and two for residential programs, and six residential team leaders who each work with four staff members. For the day service, there are six instructors and their staff. The principal heads a very well developed organizational structure of the Management Team. Descriptions of the roles of Principal and General Manager follow, with a diagram that outlines the whole team.

Principal

Responsible for directing and developing the philosophy and operation of care services at Somerset Court. Responsible for the setting of developmental aims and objectives. Accountable via the Education and Care Services Manager to the Director of the NAS working in conjunction with the Somerset Court Management Committee. Responsible for direct management and supervision of Clerical, Secretarial, and Finance services. Overall responsibility for budget. Responsible (part-time) for the promotion and development of Regional services - South West; accountable directly to the Director—NAS.

ORGANIZATIONAL STRUCTURE
OF MANAGEMENT TEAM
SOMERSET COURT

PRINCIPAL

ADMINISTRATIVE
SUPPORT SERVICES

GENERAL MANAGER/CARE SERVICES

Assistant Manager Unit Team Leaders Support Services
Residential Care   Day Care Services
Services

General Manager

Responsible for the co-ordination of the individual care program for all residents, in all areas, in line with overall objectives of Somerset Court and the National Autistic Society. Responsible for the management and supervision of all care services and the supervision of the Assistant Managers, all residential and day care staff, and daytime support services staff. Chairman of Heads of Departments meetings and Heads of Department/Team Leaders meetings. Responsible for presenting review reports to Management Committee. Acting Principal in the absence of the Principal, (i.e., has responsibility to maintain all services). Accountable to the Principal.

In Ireland, too, the director's role is to plan, develop, and finance all aspects of the project. All other professionals are employed as determined by the specific needs of the program.

The organizational structure of the German program is as follows. The director of Hof Meyerwiede is president of HAK Bremen, which owns the farm, is caretaker of the facilities, and operator of the program. The staff is employed, paid, and controlled by the board of HAK. The director is responsible for the policy, the fundamental purpose, the therapeutic orientation of the community, hiring and training of the staff, and interfacing with public agencies.

The director doesn't actually work in the farm community, but he is a non-profit-member of the board of HAK. He cooperates with the manager, who is a member of the staff. Each co-worker has a specific job such as responsibility for weavery, animals, or therapy, and each is responsible for a specific resident's needs, program, and links with parents. The staff must do two kinds of work: "social work" in the house for early or late service, as well as one's special job as, for example, farmers or weavers.

Professionals employed at Hof Meyerwiede are: seven social pedagogues (one of whom studied to be a farmer); two working therapists; one weaver; one teacher of domestic skills; and seven conscientious objectors.

Residential Programs

Settings are rural, usually on spacious and uncrowded acreage and often among farming neighbors. Somerset Court is three miles from the nearest population center set on twenty-six acres of land. There are four separate residential bungalows, a main building, and three out buildings. Dunfirth has five homes and out buildings on seventy acres of farmland. It is difficult for the program planning of staff and Boards of Directors to keep up with the rapid growth of these programs. For example, the Irish tell us that:

> The first young autistic adults came to live at Dunfirth in 1982. They were housed in the original farmhouse, which was retained and adapted to its new purpose. A second house was built and occupied in 1986, and two more are under construction. A social training room was constructed also in 1986, and a manager's residence in 1987. A current project is the construction of two growing tunnels for the market garden, together with associated buildings and stores.
>
> The development already includes a market garden, and we have begun a scheme for the planting and coppicing of willow trees, to act as a self-renewing source of fuel.

Hof Meyerwiede is in a rural setting which is integrated organically into a very small community of Grinden near the river Weser. The nearest town Etelsen is five kilometers away, the next largest, Achim is ten kilometers while Bremen is thirty kilometers away.

> Hof Meyerwiede originally was a farm with one large farmhouse, a barn and several stalls. Reconstructing these two buildings has produced two units, each for five or six adults where each adult has his own room. The large farmhouse includes a weavery.

And La Garriga is on the outskirts of a village where city people traditionally spend the summer, one-half hour outside of Barcelona. After a school had been created in Barcelona in 1976, the first country home was bought and remodeled in 1982 for education of children as young as five. As the children grew, the program expanded. Another villa was purchased in 1983 to become the first residential dwelling to be used for diagnostic purposes, to treat acute crises and specific behavior problems (sleeping, eating, aggression), and to relieve the stress on parents. Children could remain there two or three evenings each week. This partial residence was closed down for two weeks each summer and during the Christmas holidays.

Currently, La Garriga offers a spectrum of services. The school is for those under age sixteen, although some may stay beyond that age. An occupational center offers daily work opportunities to those over age sixteen, and the residence has expanded. There are now twenty beds, arranged in dormitory style where any of the forty children and adults with autism can stay temporarily for various lengths of time.

Programs

The programs are the harvest of all the early planning by parents and administrators. All of the centers either have been committed or are currently acknowledging their commitment to the long-term care and educational-vocational welfare of these adults with autism. There may, of course, be some exceptions to this general operating policy as options to move into more independent placements become available. The unique range of abilities and needs of this group requires careful and thoughtful program planning and intervention strategies. The English program specifically addresses the Triad of Impairments demonstrated by its clients by paying most attention to their social, communication, and ritualistic needs. It also targets hygiene, domestic skills, interpersonal, and educational needs in their training.

A communication skills unit operates within the day services, and a total communication environment is maintained at all times. Total Communication as implemented at Somerset Court and throughout the country refers to methods of communication incorporating a range of tools. Non-verbal exchanges might include communication boards using Bliss Symbols or computers. Residents use a touch screen to run computer programs, with some spending three to four hours a day at this task. These skills can generalize to the work environment as in the garden where a desktop publishing program is used to print labels or signs. Plans are in place to create a centralized communication facility with more computers available. Communication difficulties occasionally lead to humorous misunderstandings, according to staff:

> One resident was becoming distressed and kept repeating "the cows are here, the cows are here." Staff tried to reassure her and calm her down, thinking her chant was a meaningless perseveration, but she was inconsolable. When one of the cows that were passing by on their way to grazing land stuck its head through our front door, we understood.

Behavior management programs are only used in specific cases, based on multi-disciplinary team decisions which include the psychologist.

The Irish program sees the community-based rural setting as particularly appropriate for people with autism. It has developed an organic horticulture program that provides a full range of tasks from planting of seedlings to selling of produce. Within this context, each resident is assessed and prescribed an individualized program with specific goals and priorities. Staff work individually with residents to develop their designated skills as completely as possible.

When behavior is considered "challenging" at Dunfirth, consultants are called upon and a full medical and psychological assessment is carried out. Baseline data is collected and behavior improvement programs are created and implemented.

To improve future employment options for its trainees, the Dunfirth Community has formulated two innovative training projects. The first, the Dunfirth Enterprise Training Project, has been funded by the European Social Fund and involves eight young adults in a two-year, foundation skills training course. The trainees passed assessments and interviews by the National Rehabilitation Board to gain access to the training program.

> Dunfirth Community is committed to securing and imparting skills, knowledge, attitudes, and behaviors required by trainees toward occupational integration.

To further these goals, Job Match is the Irish Society for Autism's current Horizon Project proposal for "an action research project . . . to train persons with autism so they can avail of supported employment within the horticulture sectors open market." This would be the first opportunity in Ireland for autistic adults to enter the labor market and have the opportunity to reach toward financial independence, and further community integration. The project plan encompasses specific training of job coaches who would work with the initial group of eight trainees in local horticulture employment and training modules to address their social, communicative, vocational, and personal skills.

The research component of this venture would include extensive data bases and on-going documentation and evaluation of ability and training programs. It is hoped that results will be applicable to the occupational integration of other adults with autism in Ireland as well as in other European countries.

Medication policies are strictly controlled at Dunfirth. "Except as part of a specific program in a well controlled situation with parental approval," according to the director, "medicines are prescribed for therapeutic purposes only and not for restraint." Medication issues are approached with the advice and counsel of medical professionals as are any special dietary problems. Staff are trained, however, to provide and manage the general diet and nutritional needs, and include meat and vegetables produced organically on the farm in daily menus.

Program planning at Hof Meyerwiede includes these specific goals and objectives: a therapeutic environment, a specific individual educational plan written for each resident every six months, meaningful and necessary work, variable tasks according to the biologically determinated rhythm of nature, normalization of behavior, self-care independence, and communication skills necessary for living in a rural community.

The typical educational program at Hof Meyerwiede consists of two parts: 1) Analysis of previous goals and objectives to understand reasons for failure or success; 2) Proposed goals, objectives for the next half year in the following areas: self-care, independence, motor skills, communication/socialization/language, behavior problems, work/vocational behavior, leisure skills.

According to the director, Hermann Cordes, the Germans use behavior modification principles as modified for "natural settings": "The staff is trained to observe the actual behavior of the residents caused by the conditions of the situation, specific experiences before, or consequences. If inappropriate behavior persists in a specific situation we try to alter the underlying conditions. If the resident has problems with a complex working-task we establish a sequence of smaller steps."

Staff try hard to improve communication skills of residents. The activities throughout the day are verbally described. Residents are required to speak in whole sentences, using meaningful words or signs if they wish anything. Beside the "Communication training in natural setting" some of the residents are working with special communication programs. There is no medication used at all except for controlling seizures and physical illness.

Program planning in the Spanish setting is focused on "the needs of the autistic person and their family." The model is integrated overall with the therapeutic work and therapeutic temporary residences as interaction components. Individualized programs are created for daily activities, for behavior management as needed, and for any pharmacological treatment. Medication is limited to only that which is necessary and essential, while the diet at La Garriga is typical of the region.

Availability of professionals for consultation is variable, but a definite part of the staff and training component. Somerset has psychiatrists, physicians, and psychologists available through the National Health Service and specialist psychiatric and psychological services through N.A.S. Ireland also has formally established relations for consultation or referral with physicians and psychologists, and informal liaisons with psychiatrists and speech and language pathologists. Germany has psychologists as part of the staff and physicians may visit, but there are no regular consultants. In Spain, psychiatrists perform assessments on a regular basis and physicians are there as needed. However, psychologists are an integral part of the staff, just as the teachers are.

The program leadership of these centers does not operate in a vacuum. At Somerset Court the Principal reports directly to the National Autistic Society. The Manager at Dunfirth reports to the Director who is also Executive Di-

rector of the Irish Society for Autism. He in turn is responsible to an Executive Committee. The society gives its full
support to the projects. In Germany, the Manager reports to
the Director, who in turn is President of the HAK Bremen,
the parents' association. In Spain, the Manager of the Center is responsible to the Management Board, which in turn
is responsible to the Assembly.

Admissions criteria and procedures vary a bit from country to country. At Somerset Court families learn of services
through the National Autistic Society headquarters where
vacancy listings are circulated. Referrals can be made
through local social services. Criteria for admission include:
1) a diagnosis of autism or related disorder, 2) the potential
to benefit from the services offered, and 3) the absence of
any other appropriate services. Clients represent the full
range of individuals with autism. No waiting list is maintained, and the national headquarters is notified when a vacancy exists.

In Ireland, Dunfirth's program is advertised in the Irish
Society for Autism's Awareness projects and is presented at
meetings and through publications. Application can be made
directly by parents, or referrals might come from local
health boards. Selection is based on DSM III-R criteria for
autism and severe autistic-like problems. Dunfirth tries to
keep a balance of abilities in the community, but preference
must be given to those within its catchment area.

At Hof Meyerwiede usually the parents are members of
HAK and their children have previously been in the two
other institutions of the Bremen Project. Hof Meyerwiede is
known in Bremen and the vicinity through a governmental
publication, and elsewhere in Germany because of publications about the Bundesverband HAK.

Admissions is dependent upon these factors:

1. Diagnosis of early childhood autism;
2. Agreement of the parents to cooperate with the autism community and to do some work; and
3. Admission by the Government.

Residents could be asked to leave if, after having passed
through a special training they are not willing, or not able,

to do any work on the farm. Moreover, if several aggressive acts against residents or staff occur, subsequent to attendance at therapeutic programs designed to help a resident, they could be returned to their former setting. To date, this has not occurred.

The majority of the eleven adults with autism at Hof Meyerwiede are severely disturbed. Only five of them are able to speak in sentences, and only two of them are functioning on a "normal" level.

La Garriga is made known through public and private agencies concerned with mental retardation and developmental disabilities. Candidates for admission must meet criteria for severely affected autistic persons and must, in turn, accept the program of the center. They gain access through a diagnostic service and are admitted as openings become available. La Garriga is considered an official national team for the diagnosis of autism. There are no exclusionary criteria.

Staff

Staffing patterns vary with respect to degree of professionalization, staffing ratios, part-time versus full-time employment, degree of relevant prior college level education, and amount and type of professional consultation readily available.

Staff at Somerset Court are currently on a split-shift schedule. During days and evenings, the ratio of residents to staff is 3:1. At night it is 7:1. Some pre-service training is available with on-going day training sessions on selected issues for those employed. Formal supervision for staff members is provided at monthly meetings. A job description of a Residential Social Worker, Grade One assigned to night care is included in detail below.

The Dunfirth program consults formally with physicians and psychologists, and has an informal arrangement with psychiatrists and speech pathologists. Work schedules vary according to the various job descriptions, but a great deal of individualized attention is available for the residents. In-

SOMERSET COURT

Job Description

Post Title:	RESIDENTIAL SOCIAL WORKER GRADE 1 (NIGHT CARE)
Grade:	NAS Scale Point 7-11-14
Work Area:	SOMERSET COURT - all areas
Job Purpose:	To safeguard the welfare of the residents by appropriately attending to their needs, referring to Night Care Team Leader should on-call staff need to be contacted.

DUTIES AND RESPONSIBILITIES:

1. To safeguard the welfare of residents, in doing so contributing to the high standards of professional care offered to the residents within the "care-team" concept.

2. To seek guidance and advice from Night Care Team Leader when necessary.

3. To check on any individual residents as appropriate.

4. To provide maximum support and safety to all residents appropriate to their period of duty.

5. To maintain appropriate and concise written records of relevant dealings or contact with residents or incidents during each period of duty.

6. To work closely with all other staff to promote the individual development and care of all residents.

7. To be flexible in providing relevant cover to other areas when required by Assistant Manager, in order to maintain maximum supervision to all residents.

8. To participate in staff development and training programs as required.

9. To assist in fostering and developing contacts within the local community.

10. To ensure that conduct within and outside the Court does not conflict with the professional expectations of the National Autistic Society.

11. Any other duties as required.

And such other duties as are within the scope of the spirit of the job purpose, the title of the post, and its grading.

structional staff is present one-on-one, while in social and recreational programming there are two or three residents for one staff, depending on ability levels of the residents.

It is important that staff have previous experience in care work for persons with autism. Some are credentialed as registered nurses in Mental Handicap, a desirable but not essential requirement for employment. In-service training is on-going in areas of behavior management, safety, first-aid, epilepsy, and autism. Senior care workers on each shift offer direct supervision for staff who work with them.

There is a 2:1 ratio for day and evening staff at Hof Meyerwiede, so that four residents are working with one professional staff member and one conscientious objector. There are three shifts for staff: 7.00 - 14.30 early service; 14.0 - 21.30 - late service; 21.30 - 7.00 night service. Each member of the staff has to participate in pre-service training, which is conducted by a psychologist who works as a supervisor. (He is leader of the "Ambulance of Autistic Children."). Supervision is conducted by the "scientific counsel" of the setting: a psychologist and pedagogue, both of whom have had therapeutic experience of more than fifteen years.

In-service training:

1. Supervisors observe the daily routines/working activities, especially if there are behavior problems.
2. Supervisors participate in and structure the staff discussion concerning individual learning goals.
3. Supervisors participate in the weekly staff sessions, especially if behavior programs are discussed.

At La Garriga psychologists and teachers are part of the staff while psychiatrists are consulted for regular assessments. Medical doctors are available nearby as needed. Staff members work on rotating shifts to cover services twenty-four hours a day, seven days a week. They have Master's, or at least Bachelor's degrees, and are presented with continuous theoretical and practical training while they are on the job. Their supervision is described as "orderly technical management." Each educator is responsible for the clients.

Record-keeping practices and legal requirements vary extensively although there is a common core of concern for each resident's privacy and confidentiality. British statutes require extensive recording of issues related to program evaluation, staff employment, resident assessments, health, and accidents. Additional records are kept by decision of the Somerset program. Confidentiality of case material is insured through contractual agreements with those hired and by well-maintained physical security of charts.

In Ireland, there is no legal obligation to keep records. By choice, daily reports are written. All confidential documents are stored in the central office and are accessible only to authorized personnel. In Germany, although there are no legal obligations in this regard, the staff at Hof Meyerwiede keep "farm-books" with daily records for each home and "resident-books" in which each staff member must describe one resident each day. Learning programs are formulated for each resident twice yearly; individualized behavioral programs are created when needed, and work programs with specific goals and steps are maintained. The Spanish management must meet record-keeping requirements of the Catalonian government. All information related to autism and its problems is recorded in individual dossiers. There are only a few people who have access to these data.

Community

All of the centers foster interaction with the surrounding communities to the maximum extent feasible, acting on their belief that isolated farmstead communities in which residents are set wholly apart from mainstream life are not in the residents' best interests, nor in the interest of those in the surrounding community. Residents at Somerset are taken to town for shopping trips and for a range of personal errands. They enjoy local celebrations, fairs, and other public events. Townspeople stop at Somerset Court to buy products from the horticulture, plant, craft and woodworking programs, or to attend open houses and festivals. Staff members reach out to consult with external agencies and to offer training; they also attend training workshops offered through related organizations.

While leisure and recreational opportunities for residents abound, there are very limited vocational options beyond the Somerset environment. Relationships with parents are maintained. Visits are permitted either at Somerset Court or at home with parents on weekends and holidays. Parents can avail themselves of short-term respite services and students actually stay at Somerset Court during their assessment period. Since the National Autistic Society movement has been led by parents, they have continued to be involved in programming efforts for those with autism throughout England.

Dunfirth, too, maintains close ties to the outside community with a range of social and recreational activities including local functions and ball games, bowling, swimming, shopping, and dining. Residents go camping, cycling and caravaning, and attend musical events, discos, and concerts. There are planned holiday trips for small groups of residents and staff. Visitors to the community purchase products or stop by informally for information, while others attend open houses throughout the year. Families and friends are encouraged to visit and parents stay closely involved with the program. All are welcomed at social functions within the community, including birthday celebrations, Christmas, Halloween parties, and occasional barbecues. Regular home visits and holiday stays are scheduled.

Ireland's Dunfirth staff maintains close contact with other professionals in the field by attending and presenting training courses, and college students in child care or related fields are invited to visit the center.

The German residents go to town to visit markets and festivals and to have dinner in restaurants. They shop, go swimming, and take part in bicycling tours. Hof Meyerwiede receives families, some farmers, workmen, doctors, and occasionally other interested visitors.

The German parents are involved in the Hof Meyerwiede program in multiple ways. They participate in conferences twice a year when individual educational plans are made; they are invited to participate in one of the weekly staff meetings if the discussion is about their child; and they have to work on the farm four times a year repairing, cleaning, and painting the facility.

There is professional cooperation between the staff and their counterparts in similar settings both locally and regionally, although no workshops have been arranged thus far.

Vocational or job opportunities are not made available for the residents of Hof Meyerwiede beyond their setting, as they are considered to be placed for the rest of their lives, and are expected to continue to participate in their farm program.

The Spanish community at La Garriga makes similar efforts, so that good relations are maintained with the citizens and political officials of the town. Swimming, music, and recreational games are included in specific leisure programs.

La Garriga staff advises other centers for autism and provides an official, nationally designated team for diagnostic evaluations. Parents participate in their family member's program using the partial residential services as needed. They can also make use of the vacation therapy service that is available.

Ethical practice and treatment are serious considerations at all the sites although the degree of complexity and enforcement provisions vary considerably. Ethical standards for the English community are established in the SCA Code of Practice. Government requirements regarding ethical treatment are statute-based in both criminal and civil laws. These issues are covered in staff orientation and in ongoing in-service training sessions. The Irish Society of Autism executive committee appoints an ethical sub-committee which addresses all issues of an ethical or moral nature, including the use of sanction. In Spain, there are official legislation and regulations pertaining to ethical and moral treatment. These are adhered to in the program and compliance is enforced by inspections of state officials. There is regular training for the staff regarding these rules, as well as on-going supervision by the management and school council.

Almost all of the clinical and anecdotal evidence, the program reports, and the parent responses suggest rural, residential settings are effective and fulfilling living environments for many adults with autism. Who fits best in these places? Who doesn't? Is it possible to break down or isolate those components of the farmstead environment which contribute most to a positive outcome? Is it staff, philosophy, farm atmosphere, horticulture experience, constant attention to their needs, or education?

By way of summarizing the current situation in these four settings, here are some general observations and opinions reflecting their similarities and differences:

1. All might consider connecting with more professionals at the nearest universities or medical schools for research and evaluation perspectives and consultation.
2. Funding issues are a continuous challenge as all directors prepare yearly budgets that must be approved by their respective Board of Directors and usually submitted to their governments.
3. All encourage some degree of continued family interest and involvement, so weekends and holidays at home or family visits to the center are common.
4. In some places, work staff and care staff are separate groups, and in others their roles are crossed.
5. These communities plan to grow but they are not keeping up with their respective country's needs.
6. Activities offered in each setting include horticulture, farming, recreation, creative arts, educational programs, life-skills, and vocational projects.
7. Training requirements of staff differ among the settings, ranging from several years of professional training to staff selection based on natural interests and abilities.
8. These programs do not have built-in systematic research and evaluation components.

Future Plans and Needs

Plans for the future vary among these four settings. Most plans appear progressive, incremental, and gradual rather than utopian leaps. Ireland's current growth projects do seem quite substantial, however. Somerset Court hopes to restructure its focus of work towards a more specialized and community-based service. This would include the development of satellite units for both living and working. They want to reorganize their staff team structure, their IPP system and some of their practice issues as well.

In recent years, the National Autism Society has become a more centralized organization, coordinating activities in the four adult units, ten schools, and thirty facilities for those with autism throughout Britain. Current guidelines, policies, and procedures are more in line with research findings in the field, and approaches are becoming more sophisticated, and more uniform across settings. As a result of this leadership, Somerset Court is making important changes in its programming. Where residents were free to roam around the safe grounds, there will be more effort made to engage them in interactions and activities. At the same time, the range of their activity choices will expand and programming will become more flexible for each adult. Rather than just one or two activities each day, there will be the possibility of several if needed.

The Principal envisions the continuation of vocational projects like printing, weaving, wood-work and horticulture, but hopes to enrich these experiences with the addition of six new staff specialists who will add elements of communication, social interaction, and imagination—the Triad of problem areas in autism—into these settings. He hopes these teachers will more specifically address the core problems of autism in individual sessions outside of the work environment as well. The goal is to improve communication and behavioral repertoires in order to increase real-world opportunities for residents.

He has observed that most work has been carried on in groups at Somerset, but in fact, best results are achieved with more individualized attention. To this end he is hiring additional staff who have had experience with autism, teaching, and developmental work.

Ireland's Dunfirth project is physically expanding. They are building residential houses (in town) that will accommodate up to twelve more persons with autism and a language laboratory. Their other plans for the future are very concrete and specific:

> In time, the community will be a home for thirty-six autistic adults. We need, as well as the houses under construction, two additional houses where the more advanced residents

can live in greater independence. We badly need communal facilities, an assessment center, a hydro-therapy pool, workshops and bakery, accommodation for visiting parents and a shop/exhibition space in which to sell our products.

One new living arrangement will be a community residence about one-fourth mile from Dunfirth; a four bedroom bungalow on one-half acre of land where a housemother will live with her family. Four adults will move there from Dunfirth to lead more independent lives. While they reside in this more conventional home environment, they will continue to work at Dunfirth.

Other work options being developed include satellite market garden and horticultural enterprises in near-by towns. Contracts are being prepared that will allow Dunfirth to supply plants to factories and offices and then to provide mobile crews to service those plants. Eventually they hope to purchase a retail outlet in a more highly populated area on the outskirts of Dublin where they will sell their own products.

Hof Meyerwiede expects no changes in the near future although they want to develop more agricultural and horticultural activities. They want to have more animals, to be more self-sufficient, and to sell some of their products in the local green-markets.

They want to admit additional adults and open another home less than ten kilometers away for six to eight higher functioning residents who would learn to live more independently, be more self-contained, but still work at the farm. Last, Hof Meyerwiede wants to organize workshops to train staff who work in other settings for adults with autism.

Currently, their new workshop for wood-work and repair is being opened, and their contemporary treatment and education concepts are being organized and written. The director finds, too, that "Most of the residents need too much help—a too high resident-staff ratio. They should work more independent with lesser help."

La Garriga is continuing with its natural evolution as its students reach adulthood. The next plan is for a long-stay residence adjacent to the present property. Staff hope for more economic stability in financing their project and would like to see more definitive psychiatric planning that would focus on autism.

Whatever their beginnings, as they approach the 21st century these novel programs for adults with autism might emphasize: 1) the latest research on treatment and education, 2) promising experimental medications (Berney, 1992), 3) holistic mind-body approaches, and 4) contributions from all the human service professions. At the same time, Hof Meyerwiede, Somerset Court, Dunfirth, and La Garriga need to codify their knowledge and experiential wisdom of "what works" for adults with autism. Hof Meyerwiede is now completing a research project called "Special Programs for Autistic Adults Living in a Farm." This project consists of a professional paper as well as a demonstration videotape. Accrued expertise needs to be codified in such a way that it can be emulated elsewhere, then improved upon, and readily passed on to new generations of parents, professionals, and teachers. Creativity, originality, and boldness must stay alive despite future movement toward coordination, comprehensiveness, and cooperation among settings and countries.

Finally, the role of culture, geography, and religion might be examined in relation to the farmstead model (see Crago, 1992): Does the degree of government support, or the use of "professionals," reflect cultural influences such as the democratic tradition and feelings about arbitrary political authority? Do these settings reflect their cultural stereotypes at all—the melancholy, romantic, fatalistic Irish, the gritty and determined English, or sunny Spain where all is supposedly happy and pleasant, at least until tomorrow?

Some might see the organized and planful Germanic spirit at work in this stepwise programming: The regional society Hilfe fur das autisticshe Kind Bremen (HAF) has created projects in a stepwise fashion for those with autism since 1975. The first was a special class for children with autism, followed in 1977 by an ambulatory center for others with autism, and Hof Meyerwiede in 1988. This three-stage plan was created to continue a similarly structured environment for these children as they grew, since the government of Bremen had no appropriate facility for this older population.

A World Health Organization (1989) working group has published its report in a booklet titled "The Development of Mental Health Care in Primary Health Care Settings in the European Region." The European Region here included Spain, Germany, and the United Kingdom (as well as Holland and Denmark). The focus was not on developmental disabilities like autism, but the report made a strong case for development of community-based mental health programs. It emphasized that changes ". . . are making it possible for an increasing number of population groups to gain access to community-based care, preventive measures, health promotion, and support for those affected by long-standing chronic or disabling disorders" (pp. 2–3). Elsewhere, Van Bourgondien and Elgar (1990, p. 306) remind us, however, that with respect to residential care for adults with autism: ". . . the success of these specialized programs has yet to be documented empirically. . ."

In this WHO reorientation of programs, services, and prevention, the relationship between consumer and provider is highlighted. That means parents, volunteers, and peers will be significant in this new model as they assist and mediate between both adults with autism and professional care providers. Community social support and self-help groups will be recognized and given more credibility.

The recent International Association Autism Europe Survey of Adult Autism (1991) re-emphasizes how much unfinished business there still is in the treatment and education of these adults. Spain, Ireland, Germany, and England were among the twelve countries included in the survey. The survey admits to limitations in scientific validity, but does cover key areas such as diagnosis, care, living arrangements, social life, legal protection, and so on. The authors report that:

> In conclusion, we can say that in the areas of social and legal protection the position is generally acceptable. In contrast, in the areas of diagnosis, and in particular, specialized care and reception facilities, the situation ranges from serious to very serious even if, here and there, innovatory experiments have been initiated.
>
> From the replies it is evident that many adults with autism are taken into care and live alongside people with other

forms of mental retardation or are mixed with the population of psychiatric hospitals or - unable to find placement elsewhere - are forced to remain in the family home (p. 7).

Based on other data and clinical evidence, Van Bourgondien and Elgar (1990, p. 305) agree: "The majority of autistic adults continue to live at home with their relatives, and the degree of support services varies considerably from area to area."

Spain has an acceptable situation in indices of social life, social protection, and legal protection according to the 1991 survey, apparently not true in all of these social areas in Germany, England, or Ireland. England appears to have an acceptable situation in measures of both diagnosis and care and Ireland in diagnosis; while in Spain the situation in both diagnosis and care is called very difficult, and in Germany it is termed very difficult in care.

While proponents of integration assert the value of community life and work, the realities must be considered. The latest comparative survey of the European Community asserts with respect to employment (Demesteere and Buggenhout, 1992):

In Germany no specialist workshops for adults with autism exist. (p. 175)

No specialized provisions for the employment of persons with autism are available in Spain (p. 176).

In Ireland, the only vocational setting for autistic adults is Dunfirth, while Great Britain has a full range of employment and training services open to disabled individuals, such as adults with autism, if they are capable of meaningful work. Specifically some autistic societies established an occupational community for adults with autism or a school leaves workshop (p. 165).

International Cooperation

Given that these rural programs report to their national societies (National Autistic Society, the Irish Society for Autism and the Catalan National Association), do we need international professional standards for them? Farmsteads were established by charismatic, powerful leaders, and strong parent groups who were very well intentioned, skillful and genuine builders, but now that these programs are being copied throughout the world we might ask: 1) Do we need some kind of uniform, consistent ways to fund them (e.g., all governments contribute or all EC governments contribute)? 2) Is there a need for standards for staff, physical location, and program components?

One could easily make a case for a superordinate Board of Advisors to help establish, coordinate, and regulate farmstead communities, at least those within the European Community. Goals, funding, staffing, eligibility, and cooperative training and research could be considered for all of the EC. This would permit consideration of standards for both the physical settings and the programming for the residents. It could include research ties to medical schools and universities, and collaborative training and supervision of staff and professionals. Specialty training programs (like orthopedagogy or social pedagogy) would be fostered and personnel who were bi- or multi-lingual could move across settings in work assignments. There might be economies of scale in the purchase of equipment and supplies and the training and supervision of staff; even the establishment of common eligibility criteria and selection processes for residents could facilitate residents moving between and among the farmsteads, if necessary or desirable.

Existing organizations naturally form the framework for such a plan and provide the network of professionals, individuals with autism, and parents to lay the foundation. To begin, consider that HELIOS II is a branch of the EC responsible for the support and coordination of handicapped services. Like EC, it is undergoing change and reorganization, with a projected new format for 1993.

The European Communities Commission decided in 1970 to devote part of its social services to helping those with handicapping conditions. Mr. Bernard Wehrens headed the "Working for the Handicapped" group, whose goal was to create a universal policy promoting the integration and independence of those with handicapping conditions. Such social and economic integration was considered an important aspect in achieving a single European market in 1992.

HELIOS I was created in April, 1988, as a project working for those with handicapping conditions in the European community. Its aim was to promote their educational, economic, and social integration within the community. It succeeded in stimulating the exchange of technical knowledge and information among the twelve-member countries.

Now on the horizon is HELIOS II, scheduled to run from Spring 1992 to 1995. From the discussion group of thirty non-governmental organizations (NGO's) concerned with a wide range of handicapping conditions, and a smaller liaison group, have come goals for those who are more dependent— those with severe mental, physical, and multiple handicaps.

Proposals focus on areas of family support, early prevention, stimulation and intervention, child and adolescent training and schooling, employment training, work settings, activities of daily life for adults, housing and mobility, leisure and participation in social life, and independence in general. Legal and ethical protections are targeted as well.

Autism-Europe is the coordinating body for efforts throughout Europe by parents and professionals to expand understanding of, and provisions for children, adolescents, and adults with autism. It is concerned with research, education, professional training, and vocational or job training. Autism-Europe is an international association formed in 1983 which currently brings together thirty national or regional associations of parents of people with autism in seventeen European countries.

Its functions at a monitoring level are:

- to have autism recognized as an established mental handicap, a permanent developmental disorder;
- to look after the interests of people with autism for the whole of their lives in order to obtain appropriate treatment, education, and administrative and judicial considerations;
- to press for these demands with governmental and intergovernmental organizations.

Autism-Europe enjoys consultative status within the Council of Europe in Strasbourg and benefits from the support of the European Commission in Brussels. It is a member of the dialogue group of the Non-Governmental Organizations with responsibility for the future of people with handicaps. International Association Autism Europe has similar goals but represents only the EC countries.

NIFCAA, the Network of International Farm Communities for Adults with Autism, is a newly emerging body whose goals support the continued development and growth of the farmstead model for adults with autism. It exchanges information, personnel, and concepts among its members: communities in seven EC countries and Bittersweet Farms in the USA. Finally, the national autism societies in most European countries have regional affiliates which are largely spearheaded by energetic parents and therapists. These parent groups may have key coordinating roles in local autism treatment centers or programs, and may link up in creative ways with IAAE or NIFCAA as they expand.

Epilogue

Paul Shattock[2]

Western European governments are now able to concentrate on the well-being of their citizens without having to worry about a war with their neighbors. The activities of the "autism movement" in Europe reflect this new spirit of cooperation which is already evident in the fields of commerce, sport, culture, and science. The countries of Eastern Europe face immediate problems of identity and finance, but they are already beginning to reclaim their heritage in mainstream Europe. Parents and professionals involved with autism in Eastern Europe are learning from their more fortunate counterparts in the West to initiate much needed programs. At the same time a number of ideas, which have emanated from the East, are being studied carefully in the West.

One of the most convincing arguments for the existence of "autism" comes from seeing people with autism in different countries. Despite human individuality and cultural influences, those afflicted with autism exhibit almost exactly the same strange collection of behaviors wherever they live. The problems of the individuals and their families are virtually the same, and the required responses are quite similar, but each nation state has evolved its own inadequate system for coping with the challenges which autism presents.

Statutory Framework

Provided that appropriate services are available, parents and caregivers are not terribly interested in the intri-

[2]Mr. Shattock is Head of the Autism Research Unit, School of Health Sciences, University of Sunderland, Sunderland, England.

cacies of the legal mechanisms employed to provide them. There is a consequent danger of underestimating the importance of this framework and also of accepting its permanence. The importance of this statutory framework should not be ignored and its effectiveness should be constantly monitored and evaluated. Changes can be made and such improvements should be influenced by those the law is designed to protect.

The legal systems for the protection of people with autism in Europe have been critically described and compared with those systems operating in the United States by Vogel (1988), and the systems for the provision of services in Europe have been reviewed recently by Demeestere (1992). European legal systems and facilities have also been briefly compared in a recent report (1992) prepared for the European Parliament. In much of Western Europe, the legal system has been derived from the very reasonable "Code Napoleon" established 200 years ago. Scandinavian systems are based upon a greater recognition of the needs and wishes of the individual. Some would describe the British (and Irish) "common law" based system as pragmatic, but service users recognize the system as a shambles. Luxembourg appears to have one of the best designed systems for handling the problem of autism, but this is marred only by an almost total absence of services.

Recognition and Classification of Autism

Given the nature of the condition, it is not surprising that psychologists and psychiatrists were the first professional groups to be interested in autism. They interpreted and explained the condition in terms which they understood and which reflected the attitudes current at the time. Thus, early workers tended to see autism as a psychosis or mental illness resulting from some environmental insult and, in particular, poor parenting. In the United Kingdom, the National Autistic Society (founded as the National Society for Autistic Children in 1962) rejected this view in favor of an organic causation. The psychiatrists Lorna and John Wing were parents of a child with autism as were the psychologists John and Elizabeth Newson. Such pioneering parents, along with others, had the skills, experience, and force of character to state their case with authority. The consequence was that the psychoanalytical approach to autism never became the orthodox doctrine in Britain. Forceful and determined characters such as Haracopos in Denmark were able to ensure that, except in isolated pockets, such ideas never prevailed in Northern Europe. The pioneering contributions of Bernard Rimland in the United States should not be overlooked even in this European context.

In much of Southern Europe the psychoanalytical approach still dominates, although the blind acceptance of such ideas, by parents and professionals, can no longer be assumed. In some cases these differences in the classification of autism are the consequence of deeply held conviction. In other cases, for example in France, "belief" may be influenced by more worldly factors. If autism were to be classified as a "handicap" rather than an "illness," all patients so afflicted would be removed from the influence of the orthodox psychiatric services with a consequent diminution of their influence. A complete change of mind on the part of psychiatrists would require an admission of a very serious error of judgment, and such admissions are no more common among psychiatrists than politicians.

In Germany, where an insurance-based system of payment for medical treatment exists, the payments for therapy sessions for a mental illness are very much greater than for a mental handicap. The possibility of a diagnosis or classification based upon considerations other than objective, observational criteria cannot be discounted.

For reasons of cultural, temperamental, and linguistic differences, an international organization such as Autism Europe tends to be characterized by the prolonged discussion of issues, both trivial and important, before the acceptance of compromise decisions. These decisions are then recognized and supported by all members. This problem of the classification of autism is so fundamental to progress that no compromise is possible. The minutes of the early meetings of Autism Europe, when such matters were debated, make interesting reading but should be avoided by those of a nervous disposition. Participating Associations had to accept or at least live with the majority decision or quit. Nearly all Autism Europe publications are prefaced by an unequivocal statement of our view on the classification of autism.

"It's the squeaky wheel that gets the grease"--US proverb ("Those who don't ask, don't want")

The vast majority of people with autism are unable to voice their views and so it is our privilege and duty to speak on their behalf. Too often we, that is people with disabilities and their supporters, have been told what is good for us or what is in our best interests or even what we want. I recently attended a meeting with members of the groups representing people with all forms of disability within Europe. The prominent politician who was proposing some particularly retrograde changes to European policy insisted that all the delegates were wrong, that she knew best what people with handicaps wanted. All the delegates, whether ablebodied, physically handicapped, deaf, blind, epileptic, or perhaps recovered from mental illness, assured her that she was wrong, but we, apparently, did not have her understanding of our needs.

It is up to us to point out inadequacies, to state precisely what we want, and to present appropriate arguments in the right places.

Singing in Unison

A single voice in the form of a parent or professional appealing to his or her legislative representative will get a sympathetic hearing but no action. A single voice at a football match goes unheard but many small voices, in unison, can make a terrifying noise which cannot be ignored. There is, however, one pre-requisite—the voices must all say the same thing. How can we expect our legislators to take any notice of us when they are receiving totally contradictory demands? Only when we sing the same song are we worth listening to. The importance of strong national and local organizations to represent the interests of people with autism cannot be over-emphasized. I can produce no solid data to confirm this, but it is quite clear that the best and most numerous facilities exist in those countries and areas where a powerful consumer lobby, in terms of an active organization, exists. The current position in France illustrates the point. Although there exists a limited number of high-quality facilities, the situation for people with autism is, on the whole, very bad. There are many organizations all giving different instructions to their policy makers. Can we blame the authorities for not knowing what to do under these circumstances?

Obsessions

We are all familiar with the obsessions which are a feature of autistic behavior, but we see precisely these same obsessions in the provision of services for people with autism. Policy makers seem to develop a one-track mind when it comes to providing services, with their principles precisely in tune with the latest fad until its time is past and it is superseded by the next. The new fashion is often the complete antithesis of the previous one but must be followed just as slavishly. Service planners must be seen to be trendy, to understand the new ideology, and to use the latest terminology. There is also an inexplicable tendency for the latest trend to be a less costly option than that it replaces.

a) **Banishment**

One solution, which was adopted almost universally throughout Europe, was to remove people with any form of behavioral disorder and isolate them from society. This usually took the form of separation from the normal world and transfer into large institutions where many cruelties, in the name of treatment, have been perpetrated. Throughout Europe, such institutions (or asylums) are gradually disappearing to be replaced by a variety of alternative services.

b) "Integration" and "Normalization"

It is probably as a reaction to this banishment system that the pendulum has now swung in completely the opposite direction with "integration," and "normalization" being the only ideals for our programs. Such objectives may be laudable but not when forced upon those unable to cope with the harshness of life in the community. Vulnerable people, such as those with autism, can be subjected to abuse from the general public. This can extend to brutalization by physical violence or, in extreme cases, rape or murder perpetrated by the "normal" members of society. Certainly the person with autism has more to fear from society at large than the other way round. The old concept of "asylum" as protection from harm is lost to people when integration is enforced.

In Sweden, institutionalization has been reduced from 100% to zero. An attempt to establish a small community for people with autism had to be abandoned because of "exposure" in the press who branded the community as an "institution." Such slavish adherence to dogmatic principles is harmful and wrong.

Differences of opinion about what makes a wholesome, safe environment are most obvious when visiting communities in different countries. I am fairly confident that British inspectors of such communities in Holland would immediately close them down on account of perceived deficiencies in fire safety provision. I also believe that Dutch inspectors visiting Britain would close our centers down for similar reasons. It is likely that, in terms of effectiveness, the centers would be very similar, but quality of service is less easy to determine than the angle of the stairs or the positioning of electric light sockets.

The over-zealous application of regulations can, on occasions, make a farce of our attempts to create a home-like environment. In an effort to raise standards, British regulations require that only trained staff may work on the preparation of food. This is sometimes interpreted in such a way as to prevent residents with learning difficulties from preparing their own food in their own home. There is a requirement for a pay-phone in the building so that residents may phone home at any time. In most homes for people with autism, residents have free access to a telephone at any time and we would be delighted if they would use the facility. I am aware of one unit where all the residents are non-verbal but a pay phone is still required. How many "normal" homes have a pay-phone in the hall and residents who are not permitted to prepare their own food? Such silliness in the guise of improving services is, regrettably, on the increase.

The consequences of such policies and their rigid enforcement will be the replacement of large impersonal institutions by small impersonal institutions.

c) **Rural Communities**

The same prejudices are currently evident throughout the English-speaking world where great difficulties may be experienced in establishing rural or farming projects. Fifteen years ago there would have been no difficulty in obtaining registration for a farm-based community in England, and many such communities, catering to a variety of disabilities, sprang up. From personal experience I can testify that new communities are required to be very small and close to shops, public transport, and all the other necessities of urban life. Even the very successful village communities such as those operated by the Rudolf Steiner organization are suffering through being incompatible with the prevailing ideology.

There is a need for rural provision, not necessarily for every person with autism but, in the same way, not all people with autism are at home in big cities. For many people with autism, the noise and bustle of the city can be frightening, and the quietness and structure of farm life are therapeutic and non-threatening. In the country, where the pace of life is normally slower, the person with autism fits in more easily and his or her abnormal behaviors are less liable to attract attention or cause embarrassment.

There is, perhaps, a barely perceptible change in attitude developing in Europe in this respect. The evidence for the effectiveness of model rural communities such as Somerset Court, Dunfirth and "La Bourguette," and the novel integration programs they have developed, have given confidence to other groups to challenge the prevailing ideology. A number of other farming programs are scheduled to open in the next year in various parts of Europe.

A problem can sometimes arise in money-making ventures operated by farming (and urban-based) communities for people with handicaps. The fee-paying bodies insist that any profits from these ventures should result in an equal reduction in the level of the fees. There is, therefore, little incentive to develop such operations which could, for many people, be an aid to normalization. Certain rural communities have developed very sophisticated bartering systems which appear to be advantageous to both the community and (in terms of tax) to their fellow barterers. Such practices are commonplace in all rural areas but are more difficult to establish in a more industrial setting.

Standards of Acceptability

Standards of acceptability in terms of the actual treatment of people with autism continue to evolve. Any thinking person must shudder at the thought of the dehumanizing and barbaric therapies which have been used in the past. The wholesale use of powerful and inappropriate medication continues but is gradually being reduced. Gualtieri's (1992) warnings about the potential and actual harmful effects of medication have confirmed what many parents have instinctively known to be the case.

There is an increasingly strong reaction against any form of abuse of people with disabilities in Europe. Certainly some of the aversive treatments which, from the literature, appear to find favor in the United States would result in the imprisonment of the perpetrator in some European countries. It may be that the reaction has been too strong and that caregivers are unable to deal adequately with problems which inevitably arise. The law, as interpreted in some European countries, precludes the effective control of the explosive behaviors which characterize some people with autism. The formulation of rules which are comprehensible and acceptable to all is a priority.

It is to be hoped that as standards of acceptability are developed the criteria relate to the quality of the service provided and not merely to the administrative details of the accommodation or the qualifications of the staff. Such details are significant, but there is a regrettable tendency for such easily quantifiable factors to assume more relevance than they deserve.

Lack of Variety of Services

Not every individual with autism requires a residential community. Similarly, not every person with autism is best served by remaining at home. However, no country currently provides the range of services required to adequately satisfy the needs of more than a small proportion of its residents with autism.

In most parts of Europe, the social service framework would claim to offer personalized plans based upon the needs of the individual. Unfortunately, there are usually no more than one or two items on the menu from which parents and caregivers can select appropriate provision and the personalized plans have an uncanny knack of matching with the available provision. In Britain, for example, there is virtually no chance of real support for the family who are able to and wish to keep their adult with autism in the home, but there are many community-based residences where the problems of autism are understood. In Belgium there are very well developed home-based services, but communities like those in Britain do not exist.

National Legislation

Quite clearly, it is our own national legislatures which have the responsibility for deciding upon the type of services to be provided and the amount of money which will be available to finance them. Such policy-making bodies will remain the prime targets for our campaigns to obtain improved services. Politicians talk about "consumer-driven services" but in Europe, as in the rest of the world, such policy decisions tend to be influenced far more by economic considerations than by the actual needs of the consumer.

Those of us advocating improvements in service have to accept this situation and demonstrate that our policies make economic as well as moral sense. We must impress upon politicians the necessity of adopting a long-term perspective. When services are properly planned and organized, when the needs of families and caregivers are considered and when a range of services which fit the variety of needs is available, there need be no increase in overall funding requirements.

The politician, like all professionals, likes to look good to his or her peers. To do this the politician needs a good case, and good solid arguments to press that case. It is our responsibility to provide what the politician requires. The politician will need to be made aware that there is a problem; he or she needs the solution to the problem; he or she needs to be able to demonstrate that the solutions will not need substantial financial input. Where they actually save money, the arguments become irresistible.

The European Dimension

That then is the current situation in Europe. Each country is attempting to respond to service needs but for reasons of history, culture and ignorance has produced its own flawed and inadequate system. Twelve Western European countries (Germany, France, Spain, Portugal, Ireland, Greece, Holland, Belgium, Luxembourg, Denmark, Italy, and the UK) have, over the past thirty years, been forging closer political, economic and social links through their membership of the European Community. Many of the other Western European countries will probably become members in the near future, and the nations of Eastern Europe are already planning applications for membership. The "European Community" is often criticized for apparently inexplicable decisions (the classification of carrots as fruits is the example most often quoted), and is found a convenient scapegoat for the failure of national economic policies. The elected European Parliament does not itself fund services, but it is hugely important in setting standards with which national governments are directed to comply. It has been especially effective in forcing environmental improvements on national governments.

It is natural for movements such as ours to seek improvements in service provision through the agency of the European Community. The International Association Autism Europe was formally founded in 1983 under the presidency of the distinguished Belgian diplomat Jean-Charles Salmon. Under his presidency, Autism Europe was one of only very few "Non-Governmental Organizations" to be accorded the much prized "consultation status" by the Community. Since then we have worked closely with the officials and representatives of the European Community to put forth the case for people with autism.

Our efforts have included the holding of major international congresses and support for smaller specialist symposia. Parental exchange study tours have taken place and have proved real eye openers to those involved. International staff exchanges are encouraged and the publication "Link" keeps members informed of activities and acts as the Association's mouthpiece.

Autism Europe does not intend to provide direct services itself, but we do aim to help create an environment which will encourage and facilitate the creation of services by the appropriate agencies. Autism Europe is politically motivated but not in the "political party" sense. Autism Europe recognizes that it is exceedingly unlikely to change the entire legal and fiscal systems of countries and so is concentrating its efforts upon the establishment of standards, acceptable to people with autism, which can be incorporated into the statutory framework of each country. For an example, it has produced its "Describing Autism" (1992), which reflects the consensus view of autism without attempting to be a diagnostic tool.

Support from European Community Funds

The European Community has many initiatives which provide financial support for innovative projects. Autism Europe has, for many years, received such support (via the HELIOS initiative), which has been used to subsidize its activities including the preparation of the reports referred to earlier. Under this program our movement also receives support for its EDUCAUTISME project which is working to create modules for training people working with autism in all the countries of Europe.

The HORIZON program seeks to encourage international collaboration in the establishment of innovative programs for people with disabilities and is geared towards creating employment for such people. A Belgian project to support young people with autism in job placements in the community has recently been successful in attracting funding from this program. Perhaps this will constitute the "foot in the door" that autism needs for this initiative.

The BIOMED Program is concerned with basic medical research, and money is available to support collaborative research into, among other things, medically handicapping conditions.

There are many other Community-funded initiatives, but they all involve an element of what is termed "additionality." This requires that there is a clear advantage to be gained from international collaboration, over and above the sum of the contributions from the individual partners. The evaluation of the results forms an integral part of any project which gains support in this way.

Communications and Awareness

Although there is an interchange of ideas and information between professional researchers, the same cannot be said for the front-line professionals who face the problems of autism. Native English speakers are fortunate in having access to a considerable literature which covers most aspects of autism, but we have paid insufficient attention to resources and services available in non-English speaking countries. There are some superb programs and facilities in continental Europe but, beyond those countries, very little information is available.

There have been plans for the introduction of a practice-based, European journal on autism for some time. It is to be hoped that this will provide the encouragement needed to overcome the reticence of some specialists to report their successes and ideas. While it would be unfair to say that the "empty vessels are making the most noise," it is true that many of the fullest vessels are making no noise at all.

Autism Europe has its own magazine style publication, "Link," which appears in French and English language editions, with plans for German (of particular value in Eastern Europe) and, if there is a demand, Spanish and Italian versions. "Link" will disseminate ideas and information directly to parents.

"Rainman" was of tremendous benefit in the raising of awareness of autism in Europe, but there have been other notable successes. The "Hot-House Flowers" had a top three single in Ireland in 1991 with a song about autism. The Flemish group "Stef and Bob" did even better in reaching the top position in Belgium and Holland in the same year. In both cases the royalties were, very generously, given to fund services for people with autism.

One of the problems facing all those wishing to establish facilities is initial funding. In the English-speaking world there exists a tradition which encourages the raising of funds by voluntary effort. In continental Europe this "culture" does not exist and so the establishment of services is largely the responsibility of the state.

Aims for the Future

Europe is changing fast, with the realization that it is in our interests to work together towards common objectives. The main providers of services will always be the national (or regional) authorities and it is difficult to envisage this ever changing. A pan-European approach can lead to improvements in service. We have seen national governments forced to make changes particularly in the fields of environmental and consumer issues. The same will be the case with social services. It is our intention to work through the European Parliament so that the legal and moral high ground is occupied, and national agencies are required to provide the standard of service which a civilized society should expect.

The "Charter of Rights for Persons with Autism" shown in Appendix A has been presented to the European Parliament and has been well received. The Charter is going through the process of being accepted as a "Declaration" of the Parliament. This will provide some of the leverage alluded to above.

The "Charter" is a key element in our strategy for Europe. Detailed schedules, based upon these "Rights," are being prepared so that there can be no ambiguity in the minds of those responsible for service delivery at all levels. The responsibility for the determination of acceptability of practices is ours. Perhaps the chalice is poisoned but we are accepting it. Politicians, policemen, and purveyors of drugs are not equipped for this task; people with autism, their families, caregivers, and advocates are better equipped.

We will be looking for, and in time will see, the creation and availability of a full *à la carte* menu of services for people with autism so that personalized plans will have real meaning. This must include the option of rural, farm-based communities for those requiring or preferring this type of service.

As parents we are desperately keen to help our children to overcome their awful difficulties, and we should be forgiven for clutching at every passing straw which offers this hope. Many of these straws, in the form of half-baked theories or ideas, emanate from the USA, but we Europeans have plenty of daft ideas of our own. Supporters of these ideas produce selective data which demonstrates the efficacy of their own particular therapy.

It is envisaged that some form of agreed upon rating scales will be produced which are sensitive to improvements in performance of people with autism and that these scales can be applied to existing programs. Perhaps this will permit the early rejection of useless, expensive and, even, potentially harmful therapies.

Passports are no longer necessary for travel between many of the countries of Europe, and customs barriers between the European Community states are scheduled to disappear in the very near future. Unless each country does provide adequate services, consumers will exercise their rights and we could envisage people with autism receiving services in a country other than their own. It is to be hoped and expected that, with the gradual dissolution of national barriers, capital, ideas, systems, and expertise will be transferred between countries. The availability of genuine choices can only result in an improvement in the quality of services. A summer working in the vineyards of "La Bourgette" in the south of France might well be a pleasant change. Grape treading could well be an attractive temporary occupation for a young man from the North of Britain.

Conclusion

It is still, unfortunately, true that the quality and range of services offered to people with autism depend on luck. Even in those countries where the legal framework approaches adequacy, the quality of services is patchy and the children of middle class, assertive parents have the best opportunities. The same applies on the national and international scale. Only by defining the needs, establishing model schemes and demonstrating their effectiveness, and by using every means we have to influence policy can we expect improvements. Rural communities are wanted by parents and are popular with the people primarily concerned— those afflicted with autism. They will, therefore, make an increasingly significant contribution to total provision for people with autism.

It is only 150 years since the first British school for people with mental handicaps, the Islington School for Idiots, opened its doors. We have come a long way in that time but we, in Europe, still have much to do. We know what we want and we believe that by working together we will achieve it.

APPENDIX A

European Autism Charter

Charter for persons with autism

People with autism should share the same rights and privileges enjoyed by all of the European population where such are appropriate and in the best interests of the person with autism.

These rights should be enhanced, protected, and enforced by appropriate legislation in each state.

The United Nation's declaration on the Rights of Mentally Retarded Persons (1971) and the Rights of Handicapped Persons (1975) and other relevant declarations on Human rights should be considered and in particular, for people with autism the following should be included:

1. *THE RIGHT* of people with autism to live independent and full lives to the limit of their potential.

2. *THE RIGHT* of people with autism to an accessible, unbiased and accurate clinical diagnosis and assessment.

3. *THE RIGHT* of people with autism to accessible and appropriate education.

4. *THE RIGHT* of people with autism (and their representatives) to be involved in all decisions affecting their future; the wishes of the individual must be, as far as possible, ascertained and respected.

5. *THE RIGHT* of people with autism to accessible and suitable housing.

6. *THE RIGHT* of people with autism to the equipment, assistance and support services necessary to live a fully productive life with dignity and independence.

7. *THE RIGHT* of people with autism to an income or wage sufficient to provide adequate food, clothing, accommodation and the other necessities of life.

8. *THE RIGHT* of people with autism to participate, as far as possible, in the development and management of services provided for their wellbeing.

9. *THE RIGHT* of people with autism to appropriate counselling and care for their physical, mental and spiritual health; this includes the provision of appropriate treatment and medication administered in the best interest of the individual with all protective measures taken.

10. *THE RIGHT* of people with autism to meaningful employment and vocational training without discrimination or stereotype; training and employment should have regard to the ability and choice of the individual.

11. *THE RIGHT* of people with autism to accessible transport and freedom of movement.

12. *THE RIGHT* of people with autism to participate in and benefit from culture, entertainment, recreation and sport.

13. *THE RIGHT* of people with autism of equal access to and use of all facilities, services and activities in the community.

14. *THE RIGHT* of people with autism to sexual and other relationships, including marriage, without exploitation or coercion.

15. *THE RIGHT* of people with autism (and their representatives) to legal representation and assistance and to the full protection of all legal rights.

16. *THE RIGHT* of people with autism to freedom from fear or threat of unwarranted incarceration in psychiatric hospitals or any other restrictive institution.

17. *THE RIGHT* of people with autism to freedom from abusive physical treatment or neglect.

18. *THE RIGHT* of people with autism to freedom from pharmacological abuse or misuse.

19. *THE RIGHT* of access of people with autism (and their representatives) to all information contained in their personal, medical, psychological, psychiatric and educational records.

APPENDIX B

International Project
Correspondence

Medical College of Ohio Kobacker Center   **Department of Psychiatry**

419-381-4172

3000 Arlington Avenue

Mailing Address: P.O. Box 10008
Toledo, Ohio 43699-0008

419-381-3521
Fax: 419-381-3098

Child Division
Psychoeducational Service

September 17, 1991

Mogens Andersen, Director
Ny Allerødgård
Sortmosevej 15
DENMARK

Dear Mr. Andersen:

We have received information from Professor Paul Shattock and Mrs. Maria Hoffman of the International Association Autism Europe identifying your center as one of the important communities serving autistic adolescents and adults in Europe.

My husband, Dr. Norman Ciddan, and I have recently edited the book <u>Autistic Adults at Bittersweet Farms</u> which describes a successful farmstead community here in the United States. As a result of that project, our interest has been heightened in educating ourselves about, and possibly visiting, a variety of non-urban communities for autistic adolescents and adults throughout Europe.

We have several goals in mind. The most important one is to integrate our observations and knowledge in ways that will be useful to Autistic Communities abroad and in the U.S. Other objectives include writing a chapter length manuscript describing our impressions of European Communities and presenting their objectives, goals, and outcomes.

This letter is to ask, first, if you would be interested in participating in our project and, secondly, to seek permission to visit your facility sometime between April and October, 1992. There are several ways we would like to seek your cooperation. We'd like you to:

- Enter into an agreement with us to include your setting in our project.

- Allow us to visit your program for one or two days, most likely during April, 1992.

- Grant permission for us to collect video and audio tape interviews from your staff, parents, and residents when possible.

-    Prepare a written self-evaluation protocol about your
     Center.

-    Collaborate with us, or independently, write a chapter
     length manuscript describing your setting.

     We will present a Workshop at the International Association
Autism Europe Conference in the Hague next May and stay on for 3 or
4 days, so we hope to have opportunities for further discussion
during the course of that meeting and the chance to pin down the
details with you or your representative. Will you be attending the
conference?

     Please let us know what your reactions are to these ideas. We
look forward to hearing from you and as well, from the other
centers on the attached list.

                              Sincerely,

                              ane Giddan

                              Jane Giddan, M.A., CCC-SLP
                              Associate Professor of Clinical
                                Psychiatry

JG/krn

Enclosure

Medical College of Ohio Kobacker Center   **Department of Psychiatry**

419-381-4172   419-381-3521
                                                                          Fax: 419-381-3098
3000 Arlington Avenue
                                                                          Child Division
Mailing Address: P.O. Box 10008   Psychoeducational Service
Toledo, Ohio 43699-0008

October 30, 1991

Mr. R. C. Reynolds, Principal
Somerset Court
Brent Knoll, Highbridge
Somerset   TA9   4HQ
England

Dear Mr. Reynolds:

We have received your letter of September 30, 1991, and appreciate the welcome you have extended to us.

We will be setting up our visitation schedule in about eight weeks as so far our funding and other site visits have been assured. Gladly, all are very cooperative.

We acknowledge and share your concerns about consent forms and are preparing documents that we will offer for your approval. Ethical considerations and client, resident, and family rights guide our efforts.

As for the self-study, it will begin with a detailed questionnaire that we will mail to you before the end of the year. It will be the instrument that will focus our in-depth view of each center and allow us to compare and contrast programs throughout Europe. Meanwhile we would appreciate it if you would please send us any annual reports, brochures and program descriptions you may have.

We look forward to our visit to Somerset Court and the opportunity to meet you in person. Will you be attending the International Association Autism Europe Conference? If so we will be able to continue our discussions there.

Could you recommend some modestly priced double-occupancy lodging near your facility - Inns, bed and breakfasts, pensions, small hotels - and their cost? We are beginning to outline our itinerary and know that we must book accommodations well in advance.

We look forward to your response and to our professional collaboration.

Sincerely,

Jane Giddan, M.A.   CCC-SLP
Associate Professor of Clinical Psychiatry

LLP

Medical College of Ohio Kobacker Center   **Department of Psychiatry**

419-381-4172

3000 Arlington Avenue

Mailing Address: P.O. Box 10008
Toledo, Ohio 43699-0008

419-381-3521
Fax: 419-381-3098

Child Division
Psychoeducational Service

February 3, 1992

Madame Françoise Grémy, President
Sesame - Autisme
Languedoc Roussillon
38 Bd Sergent Triaire
30000 Nimes, FRANCE

Dear Francoise:

We appreciate your response so far and are pleased that you will participate in our international study of programs for autistic adults.

To begin, we enclose our International Autism Facilities Survey. Please take the time (we imagine it will take two to four hours) to fill out this questionnaire as thoroughly as possible. You may use extra paper for your responses where necessary.

In addition to the survey, we would appreciate receiving any written case studies that reflect the impact of your program on residents, as well as any formal or informal research or evaluation studies that have been done in your setting, whether or not they have been published.

Enclosed too, you will find a model consent form. We would like you to review it and critique it for us. Should we use interviews, case studies, audio or video material of your residents, families and/or staff, we would like to be sure that the form meets all necessary guidelines, ethical requirements, and has your full approval.

We would like you to return the completed survey to us thirty days after you have received it. If you have any questions you can contact us by FAX 419-531-6439 or phone 419-381-3521 (days).

Our thanks for your cooperation. We look forward to your response and, hopefully, the opportunity to collaborate in person at the International Association Autism Europe Conference in the Hague in May.

Sincerely,

Jane Giddan, M.A., CCC-SLP
Associate Professor Clinical Psychiatry

JG/LLP

Medical College of Ohio Kobacker Center   **Department of Psychiatry**

419-381-4172   419-381-3521
                                                                Fax: 419-381-3098
3000 Arlington Avenue

Mailing Address: P.O. Box 10008   **Child Division**
Toledo, Ohio 43699-0008   Psychoeducational Service

March 30, 1992

Sr. Joan Roca i Miralles, President
APAFACC
C. Sant Antoni Ma. Claret 282, A, 2n. 2a.
08026 Barcelona
SPAIN

Dear Sr. Roca i Miralles:

I want to give you a quick update on the International Autism
Facilities project. Several surveys have been completed and look
very interesting. I hope they will all be returned soon, and that
they can be discussed at the Autism Europe Conference in The Hague.
Would Thursday morning, May 8th, be a time we could meet at the
Convention individually, or in small groups, to review our mutual
interests? I'll be staying in a hotel in the Hague from Wednesday
through Monday.

Please let me know prior to the conference, if possible, and, if
you prefer, other lunches or dinners would be possible times to
meet and share.

As of the moment, I'm only going to be able to visit sites in
Denmark and the Netherlands prior to the conference. Funds have
been curtailed and the other site visits will probably be later
this year. I hope that change produces no inconvenience for anyone
and really it might be better since I'll know the "basics" of your
program from the survey prior to the site visit.

Until we meet at The Hague. I remain..

Sincerely Yours,

Jane Giddan, M.A., CCC-SLP
Associate Professor Clinical Psychiatry

JG/LLP

APPENDIX C

International Autism Facilities Survey

INTERNATIONAL AUTISM FACILITIES

SURVEY

Norman S. Giddan

and

Jane J. Giddan

Medical College of Ohio

Toledo, Ohio

INTERNATIONAL AUTISM FACILITIES SURVEY

PLEASE COMPLETE ALL OF THIS INFORMATION IN ENGLISH

Name of Center_____

Address_____

_____

Phone_____   Fax_____

Name of Director_____

Number of staff in Center_____

Number of clients/residents_____

1. Describe the basic philosophy and fundamental purpose of your Center:

_____

_____

_____

_____

2. Relationship to your country's National Autism Society:

_____

_____

_____

_____

3.   BRIEFLY DESCRIBE THE ORIGINS OF THE PROGRAM

        a.   Founder_____

              _____

        b.   Early Leadership_____

              _____

        c.   Need for the Program_____

              _____

        d.   Community Involvement_____

              _____

        e.   Historical Factors_____

              _____

        f.   Governmental Factors_____

              _____

4.   FACILITIES

    a.   Describe your setting (urban/suburban/rural)_____

         _____

         _____

         _____

    b.   Size and structure of your setting? (attach a map or site plan if possible)

         _____

         _____

         _____

5.   RELATIONSHIP WITH BOARD OF DIRECTORS IF APPLICABLE

    a.   To whom is your Center administratively responsible?_____

         _____

         _____

         _____

    b.   Describe your working relationship with the person or group listed above, their level of support for your Center, etc.

         _____

         _____

         _____

6.   ORGANIZATIONAL STRUCTURE

    a.   Describe the Director's function (or other leadership) in your setting

         _____

         _____

         _____

    b.   Describe the hierarchical structure_____

         _____

         _____

         _____

International Autism Facilities Survey   3

    c.   List each professional or paraprofessional job and provide a brief
         description for each (attach an organizational chart if available)

_____

_____

_____

_____

_____

_____

_____

_____

_____

_____

_____

_____

_____

7.   FINANCIAL SUPPORT

    a.   Total annual budget: Personnel (wages and benefits)_____

                                 Operating Expenses_____

                                   Other_____

    b.   What is the source, amount, or and percent of your budget?

         Public Funding_____
         Private Funding_____
         Other_____

    c.   What is the per diem cost to your setting for each resident?

    d.   Are budgetary support and salaries adequate?

         Yes_____   No_____

         Please explain

_____

_____

_____

_____

_____

_____

e.   Are budget support and salaries comparable to similar settings:

Yes_____   No_____

Please explain

_____

_____

_____

_____

_____

_____

8.   ADMISSIONS POLICIES

a.   Describe your client population_____

_____

_____

b.   How do clients gain access to your services?_____

_____

_____

_____

_____

c.   How do families in your country learn of your availability?

_____

_____

d.   Criteria for admissions_____

_____

_____

e.   Client disability criteria_____

_____

_____

f.   Range and severity of clients_____

_____

_____

International Autism Facilities Survey   5

    g.   What waiting list, if any, do you have?_____

    _____

    _____

9.   STAFFING

    a.   Describe resident/client-to-staff ratios for day and evening

    b.   Describe Pre-service Training required of the staff

    c.   Describe supervision available for staff members

    d.   Describe your work schedule_____

    e.   Describe in-service training for staff members in your setting

    f.   Does your Center have formally established relations with referral or consulting personnel (i.e., physicians, psychiatrists, psychologists, speech-language pathologists, etc.)?

        Yes_____   No_____

If yes, list specialties, and describe the nature of the relationship.

_____

_____

_____

_____

_____

_____

_____

_____

_____

_____

_____

10.   PROGRAM PLANNING

    a.   What are the specific goals and objectives of your program?

       _____

       _____

       _____

       _____

       _____

    b.   Describe any model projects you have implemented_____

       _____

       _____

       _____

       _____

       _____

11.   INTERVENTION AND SERVICE DELIVERY

    a.   Describe typical individual resident or client program plans

       _____

       _____

       _____

       _____

International Autism Facilities Survey   7

   b.   Describe your Behavior Management program_____

        _____

        _____

        _____

        _____

        _____

   c.   Describe staff efforts to improve Communication Skills of your
        clients/residents

        _____

        _____

        _____

        _____

   d.   What are your policies regarding medication?_____

        _____

        _____

        _____

   e.   How do you manage diet and nutrition?_____

        _____

        _____

        _____

   f.   What kind of involvement is maintained with residents' families?

        _____

        _____

        _____

        _____

        _____

   g.   Other special services provided?_____

        _____

        _____

        _____

        _____

12.   PROGRAM EVALUATION

    a.   Describe record keeping procedures (legal obligations)?

_____

_____

    b.   What kind of data and statistics are captured and how recorded?

_____

_____

    c.   Describe any process or outcome studies_____

_____

_____

_____

_____

_____

    d.   How is the confidentiality of case material insured?_____

_____

_____

_____

13.   INTERACTION WITH THE COMMUNITY

    a.   How are the clients/residents involved in the outside community?

_____

_____

_____

    b.   To what extent do people from the outside community spend time within your setting? For what purposes?

_____

_____

_____

_____

    c.   What kinds of interactions are maintained between your staff and the local or regional professional world beyond your setting?

_____

_____

International Autism Facilities Survey   9

    d.   Describe any consultation, in-service or educational workshop provided for others by your program

_____

_____

_____

_____

    e.   Describe vocational/career/job opportunities for residents

_____

_____

_____

_____

    f.   Describe leisure and recreational opportunities for residents

_____

_____

_____

_____

    g.   What opportunities exist for social and personal visits?

_____

_____

_____

_____

14.   ETHICS AND STANDARDS

    a.   Note any written ethical policies at your Center or published professional standards you follow

_____

_____

_____

_____

_____

_____

b.   Describe your procedures for training staff in ethical issues

_____

_____

_____

_____

c.   Do you have a spiritual or religious emphasis in your setting?

_____

_____

d.   Government requirements regarding ethical treatment?

_____

_____

_____

e.   Insurance standards regarding ethical treatment?

_____

_____

_____

15.   PLANS FOR THE FUTURE

a.   How do you expect your program to evolve in the current year?

_____

_____

_____

b.   How do you expect your program to evolve in the next five years?

_____

_____

_____

c.   What changes are underway now?_____

_____

_____

_____

_____

    d.   What changes would you like to see that are not possible at this time?

_____

_____

_____

_____

    e.   Is there pressure to alter your program in ways that do not please you?

_____

_____

_____

16.   RESEARCH EFFORTS

    a.   Are you affiliated with any university, college, or medical school?

_____

_____

    b.   Do you have access to library materials, books, and journals on autism?

_____

_____

    c.   What are your ethical standards (such as a Research Review Board) regarding research efforts?

_____

_____

    d.   Have you completed any research studies to date? If so, please describe, or attach summary or full report.

_____

_____

_____

_____

International Autism Facilities Survey   12

DIRECTOR'S SIGNATURE_____

_____
                                    (Type)
DATE_____

When completed, return to:

Associate Professor Jane Giddan
Study of International Adult Autism
Kobacker Center
Medical College of Ohio
3000 Arlington Avenue
Toledo, Ohio 43699
USA

APPENDIX D

Key Variables in International Facilities - Chart

	LA PRADELLE FRANCE	DR. LEO KANNERHUIS WOLFHEZE HOLLAND	NY ALLERØDGÅRD DENMARK	SOMERSET COURT ENGLAND	DUNFIRTH COMMUNITY IRELAND	HOF MEYERWIEDE GERMANY	LA GARRIGA SPAIN
ESTABLISHED	1987	1987	1982	1974	1982	1988	1983 Temporary Residence
LEADERSHIP GENERATION	1st	2nd	1st	3rd	1st	1st	1st
LIFE-LONG PLACEMENT	Yes	Yes	Yes	Yes	Yes	Yes	Yes
SITE	150 Acres	1.5 Acres	4 Acres	26 Acres	70 Acres	4.5 Acres	7.5 Acres
# RESIDENTS	47	20	15	43	22	11	40
AGE RANGE	18-38	23-36	20-26	21-46	16-35	18-25	8-35
STAFF RATIO DAYS	1:6	1:2	1:2.5	1:3	1:2	1:2	1:2
COST PER DIEM	$130	$130	$240	$178	$108	$168	$111
FUNDING SOURCES	100% Public Additional Private	100% Public	100% Public Additional Private	100% Public	80% Public 20% Private	100% Private	60% Public 40% Private
STAFF TRAINING	3-years college 2-years college	Ortho-Pedagogues 3-Year college course	Social-Pedagogues 3-Year college course	Previous experience	Previous experience in care-work	Proficient in skill areas	Bachelors or Master's Degree
STAFF SPECIALISTS	Monitors	Ortho-Pedagogues	Social Pedagogues	None currently	Nurse	Psychologist	Psychologists Teachers
CONSULTANTS	Psychiatrists	Specialists from Kannerhuis Program	Psychologist Psychiatrist Neurologist Counselors	Psychologists Physicians Psychiatrists	Physicians Psychologists (Psychiatrists Speech-Language Pathologists)	Physicians	Physicians Psychiatrists
SPEECH-LANGUAGE SERVICES	None	1 resident to Kannerhuis for services	Peripheral	None "Total Communication environment"	Informal relationship	Communication training in a "natural setting"	None

	LA PRADELLE FRANCE	DR. LEO KANNERHUIS WOLFHEZE HOLLAND	NY ALLERØDGÅRD DENMARK	SOMERSET COURT ENGLAND	DUNFIRTH COMMUNITY IRELAND	HOF MEYERWIEDE GERMANY	LA GARRIGA SPAIN
TEACHING METHODS	Skill training in the context of living and working	Partnership with staff • Behavioral therapy • Phase steps plan	Eclectic • Humanistic • Reality therapy • Involvement therapy • Environmental therapy	• Role • Mechanistic	Skill development in organic horticulture program	Behavior modification for "natural settings"	• Therapeutic • Educational
PROGRAM REVIEW	Weekly meetings staff/educators with psychiatrist	Weekly meetings Staff & residents evaluate jobs done and plan next week's work	Individual programs reviewed at staff conference every 6 months	Formal annual review of goals and objectives. Two or more planning meetings each year.	Weekly monitoring and recording	Individual programs formulated twice yearly	Individual programs formulated twice yearly
RECORDS KEPT	Comprehensive report on each resident every 3 months.	Daily notes on each resident	Records of treatment meetings	British statutes require: Program evaluations. Staff employment reports Resident assessments Health & accident reports	No legal requirements. Daily reports	No legal requirements. Daily records for each home Resident books describe each resident daily Learning programs 2x/year Behavior program as needed Work Programs	Catalonian government requires: Individual dossiers Psychological & educational assessments 2x/year Work programs Daily reports
OUTSIDE VOCATIONAL OPPORTUNITIES	Some	None	None	None	Grant proposal for satellite sites	None	None
EARN MONEY FROM PRODUCTS SOLD	Yes	No	Yes	Yes	Yes	Yes	No
PARENTS ROLE	Meetings as needed Home visits & vacations	Fading role Home visits	Study circle Home visits	Home visits	Social events Home visits	Active involvement	Active involvement Home focus

	LA PRADELLE FRANCE	DR. LEO KANNERHUIS WOLFHEZE HOLLAND	NY ALLERØDGÅRD DENMARK	SOMERSET COURT ENGLAND	DUNFIRTH COMMUNITY IRELAND	HOF MEYERWIEDE GERMANY	LA GARRIGA SPAIN
RESEARCH & EVALUATION	None	Satisfaction Study	None	None	None	Demonstration paper & video	Computerized behavior records
FUTURE PLANS	Holiday Recreation center New home in town	Two Kannerhuis residents will become day students here Create similar settings in Holland	A shop to sell products Information Center on Autism Group Home	More focus on social and language skills. Reorganize team structure Develop living and working satellites	Building community based homes Planning an assessment center, workshops, bakery, and a shop to sell products	Expand horticulture activities A home in town	Long-stay residence on site

APPENDIX E

Participating European Farm
Communities for Autism

Participating European Farm Communities for Autism

Dr. Leo Kannerhuis - Wolfheze
Jhr. Nedermeijer van Rosenthalweg 16
6862 ZV Oosterbeek
HOLLAND

Anneke van Belle-Bakker,
Vice Director
Phone: 85 33 30 37

Dunfirth Autistic Community
Johnstown Bridge
Enfield, Co. Kildare
IRELAND

Pat Matthews, Director
Pat Shannon, Manager
Phone: 40 54 10 09

C.A.T. Foyers
La Pradelle
30125 Saumane
FRANCE

Lionel Bourdely, Director
Phone: 16 66 83 91 34

Bremen Project - Hof Meyerweide
Bütower Str 19
2820 Bremen 77
GERMANY

Hermann Cordes, Director
Phone: 421 63 16 87

La Garriga
APAFACC
c. Saint Antoni Ma. Claret, 282, A, 2n. 2a.
08026 Barcelona
SPAIN

Sr. Joan Roca i Miralles, Director
Phone: 343 235 16 79

Ny Allerødgård
Sortmosevej 15
DK 3450 Allerød
DENMARK

Mogens Andersen, Director
Phone: 42 27 48 48

Somerset Court
Brent Knoll, Highbridge
Somerset, TA94HQ
ENGLAND

Christopher Atkins, Principal
Phone: 278 760555

References and Readings

Andersen, M. (1990). Ny Allerødgård (Unpublished monograph) Allerød, Denmark: Ny Allerødgård.

Andersen, M. (1992). Personal interview at Ny Allerødgård in Allerød, Denmark.

Autism-Europe Association (1992). *Link Special: 4th Congress Autism-Europe*. Villers-la-Ville, Belgium: Author.

Autism-Europe Association (1991). Holland: Programmes studied in detail. *Autism Europe Newsletter*, pp. 3–4.

Baltaxe, C. A. M. & Simmons, J. Q. (1987). Communication deficits in the adolescent with autism, schizophrenia, and language-learning disabilities. Chapter 7 in Layton, T. L. (ed.) *Language and treatment of autistic and developmentally disordered children* (pp. 155–186) Springfield, IL: Charles C. Thomas.

Berger, H. (1991). Treatment in the Dr. Leo Kannerhuis. Unpublished report. Oosterbeek, Holland: Dr. Leo Kannerhuis.

Berger, H. (1983). Autism and social intelligence: A report on the outcome of residential treatment of autistic adolescents. Unpublished report. Nijmegen, The Netherlands.

Berney, T. P. (1992). Aggression and autism. Conference presentation at 4th Congress Autism-Europe. The Hague, The Netherlands.

Bockoven, J. S. (1963). *Moral treatment in American psychiatry*. New York: Springer.

Borish, S. M. (1991). *The land of the living*. Nevada City, CA: Blue Dolphin.

Bourdely, L. (1990). Centre d'aide par le travail/hebergement foyer occupationnel. Unpublished pamphlet. Saumane, France.

Broekhuijsen, T. (1988). Hermien is autistisch. *Margriet*. The Netherlands.

Chesler, M. A. (1991). Participatory action research with self-help groups: An alternative paradigm for inquiry and action. *American Journal of Community Psychology, 19*, 757–768

Crago, M. B. (1992). Ethnography and language socialization: A cross-cultural perspective: *Topics in Language Disorders, 12*, 28–39.

Dawson, G. (Ed.). (1989). *Autism: Nature diagnosis and treatment:* New York: Guilford.

Demeestere, G. & Van Buggenhout, B. (1992). Comparative evaluation survey of structures and services in the E.C. for people with autism. Unpublished technical report for Autism Europe. Instituut voor Sociaal Recht, Katholieke Universiteit, Leuven, Belgium.

Doktor, H. & Doktor, M. (1992). Personal interview at Dr. Leo Kannerhuis in Oosterbeek, The Netherlands.

Elgar, S. (1991). Treatment settings in the United Kingdom for autistic adults. In N. S. Giddan and J. J. Giddan (Eds.). *Autistic adults at Bittersweet Farms.* Binghamton, N.Y.: Haworth.

European Parliament Report (1992). Report on the rights of the mentally handicapped" PE 146.020/fin

Fuentes, J. (1992). Autism and special educational needs: Looking ahead. Conference presentation at 4th Congress Autism-Europe. The Hague, The Netherlands.

Gerhardt, P. F., Holmes, D. L., Alessandri, M. & Goodman, M. (1991). Social policy on the use of aversive interventions: Empirical, ethical, and legal implications. *Journal of Autism and Developmental Disorders, 21,* 265–276.

Giddan, J. J. & Giddan, N. S. (1984). *Teaching language with pictures.* Springfield, IL: Charles C. Thomas.

Giddan, N. S. & Giddan, J. J. (Eds.) (1991). *Autistic adults at Bittersweet Farms.* Binghamton, N.Y.: Haworth.

Gidron, B., Chesler, M. A., & Chesney, B. K. (1991). Cross-cultural perspectives on self-help groups: Comparison between participants and non-participants in Israel and the United States. *American Journal of Community Psychology, 19,* 667–681.

Gillberg, C. (1989). *Diagnosis and treatment of autism.* New York: Plenum.

Grémy, F. (1992). Personal interview in the Hague, The Netherlands.

Gualtieri, T. (1992). New developments in the psychopharmacology of autism. Presented at the 4th Congress Autism-Europe. The Hague, The Netherlands.

Haracopos, D. & Pedersen, L. (1992). Sexuality and autism. Unpublished technical report. Copenhagen, Denmark: Authors.

Hegnby, K. (1989). Working fields of Danish social welfare workers: Their training and education of today. Unpublished report. Hindholm, Zealand, Denmark.

Hot House Flowers (1991). "The Rose." London Records. London, England.

International Association Autism Europe (1992). Describing autism. Unpublished technical report. Villers-la-Ville, Belgium: Author.

Irish Society for Autistic Children (1989). *Building a better future: Dunfirth Autistic Community.* Dublin, Ireland: Author.

Judt, W. (1991). Trip to Denmark: Inspection of living arrangements for autistic adults. Unpublished report of Federal Association. Oberhausen, Germany.

Kaiser, L. H. M. W. (1987). The workhome for autistic young people. A home to live, work and relax. Oosterbeek, Holland: Dr. Leo Kannerhuis.

Karst, T. O. (1991). Historical rationale of the therapeutic community. In N. S. Giddan and J. J. Giddan (Eds.). *Autistic Adults at Bittersweet Farms.* Binghamton, N.Y.: Haworth.

Kristoffersen, E. & Kristoffersen, G. (1992). Personal interview in Copenhagen, Denmark.

Lord, C. (1988). Enhancing communication in adolescents with autism. *Topics in Language Disorders, 9,* 72–81.

McDermott, R. A. (Ed.) (1984). *The essential Steiner.* San Francisco: Harper and Roe.

Meinhold, P. M. & Mulick, J. A. (1992). Social policy and science in the treatment of severe behavior disorders: Defining and securing a healthy relationship. *Clinical Psychology Review, 12,* 585–603.

National Autistic Society (1991). Approaches to autism: An annotated list. London: Author.

National Autistic Society (1988). *List of provision for autistic adolescents and adults.* London, England: Author.

Newson, E. (1992). Current interventions in autism: Some contrasting perspectives. Conference presentation at 4th Congress Autism-Europe The Hague, The Netherlands.

Patton, M. & Westby, C. (1992). Ethnography and research: A qualitative view. *Topics in Language Disorders, 12,* 1–14.

"Rainman" (1988). United Artists, Hollywood, California.

Reÿnen, E. (1992). Personal interview at Dr. Leo Kannerhuis in Oosterbeek, The Netherlands.

Rimland, B. (1991). Community, my foot. *Autism Research Review International, 5,* (3), Fall.

Rimland, B. (1964). *Infantile autism.* New York: Appleton-Century-Crofts.

Rimland, B. (1990). The non-urban alternative. *Autism Research Review International, 3* (4), Fall.

Rom, J. & Cuxart, F. (1987). *Aportaciones Para Un Estudio Tecnico Sobre Los Autistas Adultos Profundos.* Barcelona, Spain: Fundació Tutelar Congost.

Schopler, E. & Hennike, J. M. (1990). Past and present trends in residential treatment. *Journal of Autism and Developmental Disorders, 20,* 291–298.

Schopler, E. & Mesibov, G. B. (eds.). (1983). *Autism in adolescents and adults.* New York: Plenum.

Schopler, E. & Mesibov, G. B. (eds.). (1985). *Communication problems in autism.* New York: Plenum.

Smith, M. D. (1990). *Autism and life in the community: Successful interventions for behavioral challanges*. Baltimore, Md.: Paul Brookes.

Skovtofte socialpædagogiske seminarium. (1990). *The socio-educational training in Denmark*. Virum, Denmark: Author.

Stef & Bob (1991). "Breek de Stilte." HKM Records, Hilversum, Holland.

Steiner, R. (1977). *Rudolf Steiner, an autobiography*. Blauvelt, New York: Rudolph Steiner Publications.

Steiner, R. (1955). *Practical activities founded on the work of Rudolf Steiner*. London: Rudolf Steiner House.

The Advanced Training Institute (Undated pamphlet) *The advanced training of social pedagogues*. Copenhagen, Denmark: Author.

Van Belle-Bakker, A. (1992). Personal interview at Dr. Leo Kannerhuis in Oosterbeek, Holland.

Van Bourgondien, M. E. & Elgar, S. (1990). The relationship between existing residential services and the needs of autistic adults. *Journal of Autism and Developmental Disorders, 20,* 299–308.

Van Bourgondien, M. E., & Schopler, E. (1990). Critical issues in the residential care of people with autism. *Journal of Autism and Developmental Disorders, 20,* 391–399.

Van Bourgondien, M. E. (Ed.) (1990). Special issue on residential services (whole issue). *Journal of Autism and Developmental Disorders, 20,* 289–433.

Vogel L. (1988). Systems of representation and legal protection of the mentally handicapped. Technical Report. International Association Autism Europe, Brussels, Belgium.

World Health Organization (1990). The development of mental health care in primary health care settings in the European region. Unpublished technical report. Copenhagen, Denmark: Author.

Index